Successful Decision-making

A Systematic Approach to Complex Problems

Rudolf Grünig
Richard Kühn

Successful
Decision-making

A Systematic Approach
to Complex Problems

Translated from German by
Anthony Clark and *Claire O'Dea*

With 100 Figures

 Springer

Professor Dr. Rudolf Grünig

University of Fribourg
Chair of Management
Avenue de l'Europe 20
1700 Fribourg
Switzerland
E-mail: rudolf.gruenig@unifr.ch

Professor Dr. Richard Kühn

University of Bern
Engehaldenstrasse 4
3012 Bern
Switzerland
E-mail: kuehn@imu.unibe.ch

Library of Congress Control Number: 2005922551

ISBN 3-540-24307-0   Springer Berlin Heidelberg New York

Springer is a part of Springer Science+Business Media
springeronline.com

© Springer-Verlag Berlin Heidelberg 2005
Printed in Germany

Cover design: Erich Kirchner
Production: Helmut Petri
Printing: Strauss Offsetdruck

SPIN 11376293   Printed on acid-free paper – 42/3153 – 5 4 3 2 1 0

Preface

The executives of companies, non-profit organisations and governmental departments are regularly confronted with important decision problems. These problems are typically highly complex and therefore difficult to resolve.

The aim of this book is to support the management in successfully solving complex problems. At the center of the book is a procedure for approaching any complex decision problem. The procedure consists of steps which are explained in detail and illustrated with examples.

This book could not have been produced without the effort and the considerable talents of Anthony Clark and Clare O'Dea who translated the text from German into English. The authors address their great thanks to the two translators for their excellent work. Phuong Tu Le deserves special thanks for her effort in putting together the book by typing the manuscript and designing the figures.

January 2005
Rudolf Grünig, Richard Kühn

Brief contents

Contents

List of figures

List of insets

Introduction

In today's rapidly changing environment, management personnel, whether in companies, in non-profit organizations or within governmental departments, are constantly confronted with decision problems with far-reaching consequences. Survival and long-term success will often depend on finding the right solution.

This is confirmed by research carried out in Great Britain. In the study, 270 executives were interviewed from organisations reporting a total annual revenue of more than £200,000,000 each in the three sectors "Financial services", "Central and local government" and "Manufacturing and retail". "Almost eight of ten respondents...felt organisational decisiveness had impact on overall business agility". This evaluation of the great importance of decision-making is confirmed by the fact that the average value of the financial impact of a decision is approximately £167,000 (Capgemini, 2004).

To take the right decision is typically not a simple matter, as most decision problems are highly complex in nature. This complexity is due to a number of factors:

- The problem may have numerous dimensions, many of which can only be described in qualitative terms.
- Relationships between the different dimensions may be unclear so that the structure of the problem is obscured.
- The problem may involve more than one division or department of the company or organization.
- The problem may have a large number of possible alternative solutions.
- Future developments in the relevant environment may be uncertain.

This book focuses precisely on such complex decision problems. The aim is to provide support to management for their successful solution.

The book is divided into three parts:

- Part One provides an introduction to problem-solving methods. It first defines decision problems and then shows how such problems can be "discovered". It also discusses what is meant by rational problem-solving. Part One ends with an overview of the various decision-making procedures.

- Part Two introduces a procedure for problem solving which is suitable for approaching any complex decision problem. We begin with an overview of the whole procedure and then examine each step in detail. Part Two concludes with a wide-ranging case study which illustrates how the suggested procedure can be used.
- Part Three looks at two special issues. The first is the question of how to determine whether new information should be collected before taking a particular decision or whether the decision should be based on existing information. The second issue is collective decision-making; the particular problems in collective decision-making are discussed and suitable approaches are put forward.

A number of well-known texts on problem-solving exist which deal predominantly with the assessment of different alternative solutions. This book goes beyond this and includes consideration of equally important issues in problem-solving: problem discovery and analysis, the development of options, and the assessment of the consequences of the different options. Mathematical approaches are not seen as central in these first steps of problem-solving: the complexity of a problem typically arises from an initial lack of transparency in its structure, and mathematical models demand well-structured problems. Such approaches can therefore only be applied once the problem has been correctly structured - which is after much of the complexity has been overcome.

This book is intended for decision-makers in companies, non-profit organisations and government agencies. It is intended as a practical working tool to help them resolve complex problems. The book will also be useful to students studying complex decision problems and is suitable as teaching material in executive courses.

To be an effective practical working tool, this book must take complexity seriously and will therefore not attempt to cloak difficulty with simplifications and a lightness of style. Working through this book will sometimes require effort, although we have tried to be as reader-friendly as possible:

- Each of the three main parts is preceded by a short introduction which sets out the content and provides an overview for the reader.
- Technical terms are explained when they are first introduced. The same terms are then used systematically; in addition, when discussing the contributions of other authors we use the terms introduced here, even if the writers themselves use a different terminology.
- The book has an extensive index of key terms and concepts.
- We use a large number of diagrams to support the text.
- We have included numerous examples and the whole of Chapter Nine is devoted to the application of our problem-solving procedure to a real-life problem in order to illustrate the methodological recommendations.
- We have been careful to remove from the main text those sections which, while interesting, are not absolutely necessary for the comprehension of the recommended methodology. These sections are presented as insets; those who have an interest can read them and will also find references for further reading.

We trust that these measures will help to overcome the difficulty imposed by the demands of the subject and that our recommendations in this book will prove of genuine practical use.

Part One: Decision problems and decision-making procedures

Part One introduces decision-making. After working through Part One you will be able to answer the following questions:
- What is a decision problem and what types of decision problems are there?
- What are goal systems and problem discovery systems? How do they contribute to the solving of decision problems?
- What are the characteristics of a rational decision?
- What is a decision-making procedure and what types of these procedures exist?

There are four chapters:
- Chapter One introduces decision problems. First, decision problems are defined and then four basic approaches to solving such problems are presented. Of these we highlight the systematic and rational approach. The chapter ends with an overview of different types of decision problems.
- Chapter Two focuses on goal systems and problem discovery systems. The chapter begins by explaining why these systems are important in the discovery of decision problems. Next the various dimensions of goals and goal systems are presented. Finally the chapter explains problem discovery systems and the different types of such systems. A number of examples are given.
- Chapter Three looks at the characteristics of rational decisions. The chapter begins with an example, describing the course of a particular case of decision making. On the basis of this example, the chapter shows the requirements that must be fulfilled if a decision is to be regarded as rational. The final part of this chapter discusses the support that the science of management can provide to managers to help them to make rational decisions.
- Chapter Four, the last in Part One, discusses procedures for decision-making. It begins by explaining the most important terms in decision-making methodology and by defining what is meant by a decision-making procedure. The chapter then presents the different types of decision-making procedure and explains them with examples.

1   Decision problems

1.1   The decision problem

There are no decision problems in paradise! Paradise offers a happy, but aimless life. Decision problems can only emerge if a person or group of people - both referred to as "the actor" in decision methodology - develops a conscious idea of a desirable state. This state is often different from the current situation or may become different in the future. The actor is therefore required to act. He must change the current situation to the target situation or make sure that in the long term the target situation will be achieved.

The discrepancy between the current and the target situation does not in itself constitute a decision problem. A decision problem only arises if there are different ways in which the discrepancy between the situations can be overcome. The actor is then faced with the problem of devising and assessing different courses of action. It frequently happens that on first examination only one possible course of action is identified to address the discrepancy between the current and target situations. But in almost all situations there is more than one option. It is therefore better not to be satisfied with an initially identified course of action but to look systematically for options and to choose the best of them. In this way, the quality of the solution to the problem is usually significantly improved.

This means a decision problem has the following characteristics:
- A discrepancy between the current situation and the target situation
- At least two options for action to achieve the target

1.2   Ways of solving decision problems

A decision problem is present when the discrepancy between the current situation and the target situation can be reduced and/or overcome through different courses of action. There are a number of very different ways in which we can determine which course of action should be taken. The decision can be approached:

- purely intuitively without careful reflection about the problem
- through routine recourse to procedures used in the past
- by adopting unquestioningly the solutions suggested by experts
- by choosing at random
- on the basis of systematic rational thought supported by relevant information

All of the above occur in practice. They are of interest to business management researchers for the purposes of describing and explaining entrepreneurial decisions. This is known as descriptive decision theory (Gäfgen, 1974, p. 50 ff.). This book puts forward suggestions for the improvement of decision-making in practical problem situations rather than focusing on descriptions of decision processes of the past. Our book is therefore concerned with prescriptive decision theory (Gäfgen, 1974, p. 50 ff.).

Inset 1.1 gives additional clarification of prescriptive and descriptive decision theory and compares these two approaches to a third type of decision theory - decision logic.

Inset 1.1: Descriptive decision theory, prescriptive decision theory and decision logic

As Gäfgen (1974, p. 50 f.) shows, models of rational choice can be developed without considering real problems. These models are only thinking experiments, logical derivations from postulated assumptions, whose results are true purely in logical terms. If standards of logic are strictly observed, there is absolute certainty that new propositions derived from given axioms are correct (Gäfgen, 1974, p. 50 f.).

One can use a model of this kind to make the implications of a given assumption clear, in our case the assumption of rational choice. From the point of view of logic, these implications are self-evident, but they are often difficult to arrive at and psychologically new. A scientist will normally only abandon an assumption once he or she understands all that is - sometimes surprisingly - implied by it. Decision models show what individual rational behaviour is like and where in everyday experience rationality and irrationality can occur. (Gäfgen, 1974, p. 1 f.)

However, in addition to showing what individual rational behaviour is like, decision logic can also serve as a basis for exploring in an empirical way how decisions are made in practice. In this case we can speak of descriptive decision theory (Gäfgen, 1974, p. 52).

Decision logic can also be used as a basis for the development of prescriptive decision models. These contain instructions for action for rational decisions and fall under the heading of prescriptive decision theory (Gäfgen, 1974, p. 52).

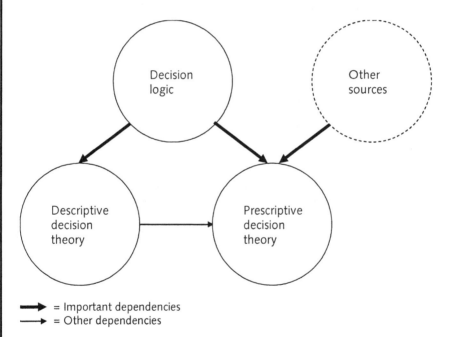

➡ = Important dependencies
→ = Other dependencies

Figure 1.1: The different types of decision research and their dependencies

Decision logic undoubtedly represents an important basis for prescriptive decision methodology. But it is not the only basis for it. To develop usable decision-making procedures, a sound knowledge of heuristic principles is required (see inset 5.1) along with practical experience of problem-solving processes. Information relevant to the development of prescriptive decision models can also be found in descriptive decision theory.

Figure 1.1 shows the dependencies between the different types of decision research.

This book concentrates exclusively on prescriptive decision theory. Since a theory is generally understood to be an explanation of a part of reality and since prescriptive decision theory contains recommendations for shaping actions rather than explanations, the word "theory" is perhaps not ideal. Decision methodology seems a more appropriate expression.

Prescriptive decision methodology focuses on systematic rational decisions. This does not mean that the authors regard executives' intuition and experience as irrelevant. Even when proceeding rationally, incomplete information on some aspects of the situation and more particularly lack of certainty over the effects of the possible courses of action, mean that the decision-maker has to fall back on experience and intuition. If - as is often the case in practice - a decision must be made under pressure, it becomes even more important to compensate for missing information with judgements based on intuition and personal experience. Sometimes it is wise to integrate purely intuitively discovered solutions in the decision-making process and to compare them with courses of action worked out systematically. This puts the search for a solution on a wider basis. Rational action on the one hand and intuitive experience-supported action on the other should therefore not be seen as opposites; they complement each other when problem-solutions are developed in real-life. The methodological suggestions introduced in this book are based on the authors' conviction that the solution of decision problems must in practice incorporate sensible use of intuition and experience.

1.3   Types of decision problem

A number of criteria can be used to distinguish between different types of decision problem (see Rühli, 1988, p. 186 ff.). Below we present the criteria and characteristics to which we will return later in the book.

Figure 1.2 gives an overview of the most important parameters and values of decision problems.

According to the degree of difficulty of the problem (parameter 1 in Figure 1.2), we distinguish between simple and complex decision problems. A complex decision problem is present if one or more of the following conditions simultaneously apply:

- The problem has many facets, some of which can only be described in qualitative terms.
- The different problem parameters are interdependent. This leads to an unclear structure of the problem.
- More than one department in the company is involved in the problem.
- A large number of possible solution-options exist.
- Environmental developments are uncertain.

If none of the above characteristics applies, the problem is a simple decision problem.

As the title states, this book deals with complex decision problems. The distinction between simple and complex decision problems is thus important in defining the topic of the book.

The classification into well-structured and ill-structured decision problems (parameter 2 in Figure 1.2) comes from Simon and Newell (1958, p. 4 f.). A problem can be termed well-structured if its solution can be found using an analytical decision-making process. Where this is not the case, we have an ill-structured problem. A more precise definition of well-structured and ill-structured is not possible here, as the conceptual basis for this has not yet been introduced. We return to the issue in Chapter 4, Inset 4.2.

Parameters	Values		
(1) Degree of difficulty	Simple	Complex	
(2) Problem structure	Well-structured	Ill-structured	
(3) Problem character I	Choice Problem	Design Problem	
(4) Problem character II	Threat Problem	Opportunity Problem	
(5) Type of actor	Single decision-maker	Collective decision-maker	
(6) Number of goals to be followed	Single	Multiple	
(7) Ability to predict consequences	Consequences predicted with certainty	Different possible consequences with probabilities for each	Different possible consequences without probabilities

Figure 1.2: The parameters of decision problems and associated values

The distinction between choice and design problems (parameter 3 in Figure 1.2) is suggested by Simon (1966, p. 1 ff.). Choice problems are problems in which the decision options are known from the beginning. For example, if there are three potential suppliers of a specialized machine, the actor has three options. Of these the actor must choose the best one. In contrast, the situation is quite different if a new company headquarters is to be built. Even if the site has already been decided upon, there is an almost infinite number of possibilities for the structure and layout of the building. The problem can only be solved if it is broken down into parallel and consecutive sub-problems so that the new headquarters is planned step by step.

From what has been said so far, the reader will probably have understood that the different categories of problem are not unrelated. Simple decision problems are always choice problems and often meet the requirements of a well-structured decision problem. Complex problems are usually design problems and are always ill-structured. **Figure 1.3** illustrates these connections.

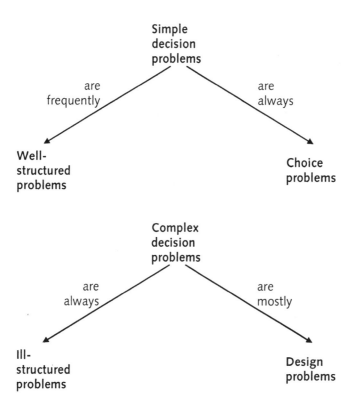

Figure 1.3: Types of decision problem and connections between them

When we speak in layman's terms of a problem, we almost always mean the overcoming of a danger, in other words (in accordance with the fourth parameter in Figure 1.2) a threat problem. In this book, the term "problem" is understood in a neutral way as a difference between a current situation and target situation. Accordingly, there are not only threat problems but also opportunity problems. Complex problems frequently contain sub-problems of both types and it is important from a practical point of view not to restrict oneself to the sub-problems representing threat.

The actor makes a decision and selects the option to be realized. Here a distinction is made between individual and collective decisions (parameter 5 in Figure 1.2). An individual decision does not exclude the involvement of other people at the problem analysis stage and in the development and evaluation of options. A collective decision exists only if a number of people are jointly responsible for selecting the option to be realized.

In parts I and II of this book, the assumption is made that the actor is an individual. However, as many important decisions are made by committees these days, collective decisions are of considerable importance. The focus on single decision makers in part I and II is motivated by a desire for clarity. To keep our discussion clear, we first present the methodological problems common to all decisions by looking at single decision-maker problems. Collective decisions throw up specific methodological questions and these are dealt with separately in Part III.

If the actor is only pursuing one objective (parameter 6 in Figure 1.2), there is a univalent decision-problem. We can also speak of a univalent decision problem if the actor is pursuing more than one objective, but these objectives have an arithmetical relationship to each other. For example, this is the case with net sales and variable costs, from which contribution margin can easily be computed. However, more often in the decision there are a number of objectives to take into account which have no arithmetical relationship to each other; this is called a polyvalent decision.

For each decision option, it is possible to predict with a greater or lesser degree of certainty its effects or consequences (parameter 7 in

Figure 1.2). For these consequences to be predicted with certainty is an exception. More frequently, features of the situation which have a fundamental influence on the consequences of the options can develop in different ways. Sometimes probabilities can be assigned to uncertain consequences, which allow the risk connected with the decision to be quantified. Decisions of this kind are referred to as risk decisions. Often, however, it is not possible to attribute probabilities to uncertain consequences because the actor has too little information. Obviously this makes decision-making particularly problematic. We speak in this case of an uncertain decision.

Six types of decision problem are presented in Chapter 5, distinguished on the basis of differentiation between univalent and polyvalent decisions and of differentiation between certain, risk and uncertain decisions.

2 Goal and problem-finding systems as requirements for the discovery of decision problems

2.1 The functions of goal and problem-finding systems in the discovery of decision problems

Goal and problem-finding systems are both important prerequisites for the discovery of decision problems. But they perform different functions, as this chapter will show.

An actor has a decision problem only if he or she has at least a vague idea of what might be desirable or of what a situation should be like. A problem is only present if (1) a difference emerges between the desired or the target situation and the current or developing situation, and (2) if this difference appears sufficiently serious to justify intervention by the actor. If more than one starting point or possibility exists for overcoming these differences, the problem can be considered a decision problem.

In management science, perceived target situations are called goals. Companies normally have multiple goals, both for the whole company and for individual functions, such as purchasing, production and marketing. These goals together make up the goal system for the business. Goal systems are a necessary prerequisite for discovering decision problems.

Discrepancies between current and target situations can be discovered ad hoc. For example, on a routine tour of the department the production manager may notice that certain machines are not running properly. Or a product manager might notice an unusually high number of complaints from clients about the quality of a particular product. Well-trained and experienced executives are certainly capable of discovering basic problems in this way. But the risk clearly remains that not all basic problems will be discovered ad hoc and that a problem will not be discovered in time for effective intervention to take place. To lessen this danger, many businesses make use of problem-finding systems which make it possible to discover decision problems systematically and to identify them at an earlier stage than would otherwise be the case. The simplest example of a problem-finding system of this kind is the turnover and cost budget; the figures of this budget are regularly monitored to ascertain whether turnovers are attained and costs kept within predefined limits.

Unlike goal systems, problem-finding systems are not a necessary prerequisite for the subsequent discovery of problems. From a practical viewpoint, however, they represent important instruments for the early and reliable identification of decision problems.

2.2   Goal systems

2.2.1   Goal systems as combinations of single goals

Goal systems are combinations of single goals. So first we must make clear what a goal is and what its dimensions are.

A goal is a perception of a desired state which the actor strives for (Heinen, 1976, p. 45). A complete goal description requires the following key elements (Stelling, 2000, p. 7 f):
- a statement of goal content or goal variable
- a statement of the required degree of attainment of the goal
- a statement on the temporal validity of the goal
- a statement on the scope of applicability of the goal

These four elements will now be explained.

Undoubtedly the most important element of a goal description is the content basis of the goal or the goal variable. The spectrum of possible goals is extremely wide. Business goals currently pursued can be divided into three broad areas: performance goals (quality, capacity utilisation, productivity, market share), financial goals (profit, ROI, liquidity) and social goals (employee satisfaction, corporate responsibility) (Stelling, 2000, p. 7 f.).

The second element in a goal description relates to the degree of attainment of the goal. We distinguish between optimizing goals and satisfying goals. With optimizing goals the goal variable is maximised or minimised. Financial goals, like profit, ROI or shareholder value, are often optimizing goals. In contrast to this, satisfying goals set a standard which must be reached. For example, a global player may stipulate a minimum level of turnover for a new geographic market. If this level is not reached, say within three years of market entry, activities in this country will be abandoned (Stelling, 2000, p. 7).

Each goal should contain a reference to time for achieving it. For example, it must be clear what the time frame is for achieving a specified increase in productivity. The differentiation of short-term, medium-term and long-term goals has become standard in business management practice (Grünig, 2002, p. 41 ff.; Stelling, 2000, p. 7 ff.).

Finally, the scope of the objective needs to be stated. The objective can refer to geographically defined units (country or region), legal entities (subsidiary) or organisational units (division) (Stelling, 2000, p. 7 ff.).

A company's target situation almost always includes a number of different elements. In reality an actor hardly ever pursues a single goal but nearly always a wider set of goals or a goal system. A goal system is not always completely precise in every respect and typically may present internal contradictions. It is therefore safe to assume that a company's perceptions of the target situation will be confused in some areas and may contain contradictory positions. A theologian friend once said that it is the contradictions that exist within human beings which shape us the most and make us unique.

2.2.2   Approaches to classifying goal systems

In the previous subsection we presented two characteristics of goal systems:
- They are often imprecise, at least in some areas
- They may contain internal contradictions

The objective of this book is to provide helpful recommendations for use in practice. So it is important to recognize the complexity of reality and not to be tempted to make simplifying assumptions.

However, in order to create a basis for addressing this complexity, we will now provide some ideas for classifying goal systems.

From a practical viewpoint, four dimensions are essential in distinguishing between different types of goals:

- Importance: Goals can be divided into categories, such as very important, important and others. Typically, however only two categories are used - main goals and additional goals.
- Scope: It is useful to differentiate between overall goals of the company and individual goals of separate units such as product divisions, regional units or functional units.
- Time: Goals can be divided into long-term (often until further notice), medium-term (2 to 5 years), and short-term goals (one year or less).
- Degree of attainment: This distinguishes between optimizing and satisfying goals

These four criteria can be applied together to structure a goal-system. **Figure 2.1** presents an example. It is a goal system with the main goal of maximizing return on equity and a number of additional goals which do not all concern the whole corporation, but only specific functional areas. With the exception of above-average product quality - according to the PIMS research, above-average product quality leads to above-average profitability (Buzzell/Gale, 1989, p. 89 ff.) - the additional goals all have a negative effect on the main goal of return on equity. However, the goals have the benefit of reducing risks and of forestalling difficulties with important partners:

- Growth takes place slowly, only in the core business and on a strong equity basis.
- Social and ecological goals promote good relationships with employees, environmental protection organisations and public authorities.

The goal system shown in Figure 2.1 is long-term in orientation. It remains to be determined what the appropriate medium-term and short-term goals for this company would be.

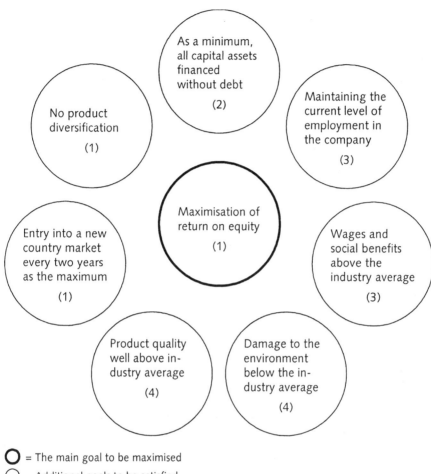

◯ = The main goal to be maximised
◯ = Additional goals to be satisfied
(1) = Corporate goal
(2) = Financial goal
(3) = Human resources goal
(4) = Production goal

Figure 2.1: Example of a goal system

2.3   Problem-finding systems

For systematic monitoring and early recognition of problems, companies develop problem-finding systems. According to Kühn & Walliser (1978, p. 227 ff.), problem-finding system can be defined as:

- subsystems of the corporate information system
- which gather, process and store information
- in order to discover decision problems and set problem-solution processes in motion (This may not be their only function).

Every business possesses a legally required tool - financial accounting. In addition to furnishing financial documentation, this can serve as a problem-finding device. However, as a problem-finding system, financial accounting is slow to provide information and set the necessary analysis and decision process in motion. For this reason, most companies set up other systems exclusively for problem finding. As well as accounting approaches, such as cost accounting and cash flow monitoring, systems are used which are specially designed to reveal changes in the environment. These problem-finding systems can highlight changes in the market and in technology as well as in the underlying legal, social and ecological conditions. They can normally reveal problems earlier than instruments which are based on internal data. For this reason, they are also known as early-warning systems.

The central component of a problem-finding system is its set of problem indicators. A problem indicator is a variable; when its value changes, the actor knows or can assume, that the change may indicate a problem (Kühn & Walliser, 1978, p. 229).

Four categories of problem indicators can be differentiated (Kühn & Walliser, 1978, p. 229 ff.):

- General goal indicators, such as return on equity
- Variables which have an arithmetical relationship with a general goal indicator. These can be called differentiated goal indicators. For example, overall turnover is a general goal indicator which can be divided into the turnover of product groups, client groups, or regions. Each of these separate values for turnover stands in a

mathematical relationship to overall turnover, so these will be differentiated indicators.

- Operational cause indicators. These consist of variables with a cause-effect relationship to a goal indicator and show problems on the operational level. **Inset 2.1** introduces indicators suggested by Parfitt and Collins (1968, p.131 ff.). These indicators reveal market problems for consumer goods before the turnover starts to fall.
- Strategic cause indicators. As the purpose of strategic management is to construct and protect success potentials, these indicators show changes in market position, in the competitive advantages in the offer, and in competitive advantages in resources. **Inset 2.2** presents strategic cause indicators for an academic publishing house.

Inset 2.1: The operational cause indicators of Parfitt and Collins

Market share is an important measure for planning and monitoring the market position of consumer goods. Parfitt and Collins developed their indicator system in order to be able to predict changes in market share and to be able to respond early in the case of a decrease in market share. It is based on four quantitative indicators:

- Quantitative market-share of product a $=$ $\dfrac{\text{Sales quantity of product a}}{\text{Sales quantity of all products in the category A}}$

- Cumulative penetration of product a $=$ $\dfrac{\text{Number of consumers who have purchased product a on at least one occasion}}{\text{Number of consumers who have purchased a product in the category A on at least one occasion}}$

- Repeat purchasing rate of product a $=$ $\dfrac{\text{Average number of purchases made by the consumers of product a}}{\text{Average number of purchases made by all consumers in the category A}}$

- Buying rate index of product a $=$ $\dfrac{\text{Average number of units purchased per purchasing act for product a}}{\text{Average number of units purchased per purchasing act in the category A}}$

All indicators relate to a certain period t, for example a month or a quarter.

The four indicators have a mathematical relationship to each other:

$$\text{Quantitative market share of product a} = \frac{\text{Cumulative penetration of a} \bullet \text{Repeat purchasing rate of a} \bullet \text{Buying rate index of a}}{100}$$

This means that if indicator values are empirically determined then the results can be validated (Kühn & Walliser, 1978, p. 237 ff.; Parfitt & Collins, 1968, p. 131 ff.).

We can now give an example of how the indicator system functions. **Figure 2.2** shows the quantitative target market share and the values for Parfitt and Collins' four problem indicators for a product group of a company.

Quarter	1	2	3	4
Target market share in units	10%	10%	10%	10%
Current market share in units	10%	10%	10%	10%
Current cumulative penetration	40%	42%	50%	52%
Current repeat purchasing rate	40%	35%	32%	30%
Current buying rate index	0.625	0.680	0.625	0.641

Figure 2.2: Parfitt and Collins' four indicators for a product group
(adapted from Grünig, 2002, p. 36; Kühn & Walliser, 1978, p. 239)

Market share alone gives no cause for concern throughout the four quarters. In contrast, the repeat purchasing rate has fallen, indicating the problem of decreasing client satisfaction. This problem has not yet had a negative effect on the turnover because an advertising campaign in quarters 2, 3 and 4 has attracted new buyers and increased cumulative market penetration. But after the advertising campaign is over, cumulative penetration will probably fall to the original level of 40%. Even if the repeat purchasing rate and the buying rate index remain the same at 30% and 0.641 respectively, market share in the next quarter will drop to 7.6%. Parfitt and Collins' indicators thus allow problems in market position to be discovered before market share is affected and the problem becomes acute.

Inset 2.2: The strategic cause indicators of a publishing company

Bigler is a German-language publisher specializing in teaching materials for biology and medicine. The sub-market for university-level books is important both for turnover and for the company's image. **Figure 2.3** shows the problem indicators used by Bigler to monitor its position in this important sub-market. As can be seen in the illustration,

- the first two groups of indicators monitor the development of the market and the positions of competitors with substitute products
- the other three indicator groups show Bigler's market position, not on the level of market share but on a level underlying market share. For example, if renowned academics begin to turn away from Bigler and publish their textbooks with competitors, this will have the medium-term effect of decreasing Bigler's market share.

The systematic and periodic monitoring of indicators, as in this example, will undoubtedly bring certain research costs. Although this must be accepted for a strategic early-warning system, the expense should not be overestimated. It is usually noticeably higher first time round than for subsequent determinations of the indicator values.

The cause indicators in this case are based on the knowledge of the managers responsible. One could also base the indicators on empirically validated cause-effect models. In practice, however, this is rarely done.

(1) The number of student places in German-speaking universities
  - for biology as a main subject
  - for biology as an additional subject
  - for medicine

(2) Percentages for compulsory and for recommended English-language course books at 10 randomly chosen universities
  - in biology courses at German-speaking universities
  - in medicine courses at German-speaking universities

(3) Percentage of the 100 most prominent academics publishing exclusively or predominantly with Bigler in comparison to the competitors
  - German-speaking biologists
  - German-speaking medical specialists

(4) The number of new books as a percentage of Bigler's available catalogue in comparison to the competitors
  - for German-language biology books
  - for German-language medicine books

(5) Average print run, including subsequent editions, for Bigler's publications in comparison to the competitors
  - for German-language biology books
  - for German-language medicine books

Figure 2.3: Bigler's strategic cause indicators for the monitoring of its university teaching materials

It is clear that early-warning systems are based above all on cause-indicators, while the problem-finding systems of accountancy are primarily general and differentiated goal indicators. The essential advantages and disadvantages of goal and cause indicators and of problem-finding systems based on them are summarised in **Figure 2.4**. The illustration shows two opposing tendencies:

- On the one hand, cause indicators and the early-warning systems based on them react early and show problems before they have escalated too far. This gains valuable time for the actor to process the problem and to apply the chosen solution. In contrast, goal indicators respond late. Accordingly the actor may be confronted with problems when it is already too late for effective measures.
- On the other hand, with cause-indicators there is a risk of a false alarm causing unnecessary expenditure on analysis and on solving the imaginary problem. This risk is practically non-existent with

goal indicators. When they react, there is a high likelihood that a decision-problem exists.

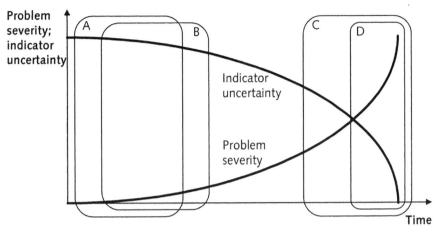

A = Strategic early-warning system with strategic cause indicators
B = Operational early-warning system with operational cause indicators
C = Accountancy-based problem-finding system with differentiated goal indicators
D = Accountancy-based problem-finding system with general goal indicators

Figure 2.4: The advantages and disadvantages of the different types of problem-finding systems and problem indicators
(adapted from Kühn & Walliser, 1978, p. 231)

3 Rational decisions

3.1 The sequence of events in decision-making procedures as a framework for rational decisions

In practice, finding the solution to a decision problem is often time-consuming. This is because a great deal of thought is required between the discovery of the problem and the choice of the optimal action. It takes time to grasp the problem, to discover meaningful approaches to the solution and to know which option to go for. It is appropriate therefore to look at decisions as thought processes and to see rational decisions as the outcome of rational decision-making procedures. We begin by showing how decision-making procedures operate and what kinds of deliberations come into play in these procedures.

Let's begin with an example of how a decision-making procedure might run in practice. Mr. Mordasini is head of production at Autotech Inc., a Swiss manufacturer of metal components for automobiles. Apart from looking after approximately 100 manufacturing employees and production planning, Mr. Mordasini is also responsible for the operation and maintenance of the plant. For metalworking, the department has a number of lathes, milling machines and drills. The production department also has equipment to polish metal parts and galvanised baths to treat the parts for corrosion damage.

On Monday afternoon at 4.15 pm, a quarter of an hour before the end of the working day, Mr. Mordasini is called to the lathes section. One of the five lathes is on fire! When he arrives, Mr. Jäk, the foreman of the section, has already succeeded in putting out the fire in the electric motor of the lathe with a fire extinguisher. An hour later the machine has cooled down sufficiently for Mr. Mordasini and Mr. Jäk to determine the extent of the damage. The motor fire has heated the lathe to such an extent that individual parts have been deformed. The two men immediately agree that the machine will never again produce parts to the required quality and the value of the machine is therefore reduced to scrap metal.

Since the lathe section is working at 100% capacity, Mr. Mordasini orders new working hours from Wednesday. Mr. Jäk must ensure on Tuesday that one of the remaining machines is worked from Wednesday on from 5.00 to 7.00 a.m. and from 4.30 p.m. to 9.00 p.m. Moreover, workers in the lathe section will have to work over-time on Saturday mornings, if needed.

On Tuesday morning, Mr. Mordasini immediately informs the manag-ing director, Mr. Kämpf, about the incident and the response meas-ures. The two agree that the machine, which was insured, must be replaced. Mr. Kämpf also believes it might be possible to replace this manual lathe which has been destroyed with a semi-automated or automated machine. Mr. Kämpf gives Mr. Mordasini the task of de-veloping and assessing the different options. He expects a compre-hensive proposal from him as soon as possible.

Mr. Mordasini begins the job immediately and defines the basic con-ditions for the new lathe:

- In recent years, the capacity of the lathe section, with its five ma-chines, was always fully used. It yielded a gross profit of 1,776,500 Swiss francs in the last year, with the five manual lathes working 220 days for 8.5 hours per day, each making 190 Swiss francs gross profit per hour. From a discussion with Mr. Kessler, Autotech's sales manager, it is apparent that additional orders could be obtained, corresponding to approximately one year's gross profit of 600,000 francs. In order not to have to make price concessions, the increase in order volume should take place gradually over three years. To be safe, Mr. Kessler and Mr. Mordasini decide to reckon on extra order volume worth only a gross profit of 300,000 francs and to adopt a pessimistic view of the increase in volume taking place gradually over three years.
- As regards the precision quality of the machine, Mr. Mordasini sees no reason to change from the previous standard of 1/100 mm.
- It is the policy of the company only to purchase and use machinery which fully meets the safety requirements of the Swiss accident in-surance company.
- Mr. Mordasini finally decides, after consultation with his superior, that the machine must be replaced within three months. It would

not be reasonable to ask the employees of the lathe section to work overtime for more than three months.

Accordingly, Mr. Mordasini contacts three producers of lathes as well as a dealer in second-hand machinery. Since the dealer has no lathes in stock which fulfil the four requirements, he is removed from the list of potential suppliers. Representatives of the other three manufacturers visit Autotech within the week and, bearing in mind the urgency of the situation, promise to send a written quote by the end of the following week.

The quotes come in on schedule. At first, Mr. Mordasini checks whether they fill the basic conditions set by him and he finds that they all do. Then Mr. Mordasini produces a table with the finance director, Mr. Wälti, as in **Figure 3.1**, showing the years of use and the financial effects for each option. The manual lathe from the previous supplier is the closest option to the wrecked machine and represents a simple replacement. The investment of 180,000 francs is covered by the fire insurance policy. The semi-automated lathe from Kunz has the same capacity as the manual machine and therefore qualifies as a rationalisation investment. Finally, the automated machine from Hinz would represent investment for both rationalisation and expansion.

As can be seen from the illustration, Option A serves as the reference option. The annual revenues and expenditures of options B and C are not fully known, but increases in revenue and increases or decreases in expenditure can be identified in comparison to option A.

Since the damaged lathe must in any case be replaced and this replacement will be paid for by the insurance company, Option A is the zero option for Mr. Mordasini. It will be chosen if neither of the other two options proves to be economically more advantageous than a straightforward replacement. Mr. Mordasini evaluates the economic effects of options B and C, as is usual in Autotech, by means of a calculation of the net present values. **Figure 3.2** shows the result of the calculations. The following points are worth making:

Options	Years of use	Investment including installation in thousands of Swiss francs	Annual difference in turnover in thousands of Swiss francs	Annual difference in personnel costs in thousands of Swiss francs	Annual difference in energy and maintenance costs in thousands of Swiss francs
A: Manual lathe from the previous supplier	8	180	-	-	-
B: Semi-automated lathe from Kunz	8	360	0	-40	0
C: Automated lathe from Hinz	6	1070	Year 1: +100 Year 2: +200 Year 3 + ff: +300	-60	+10
Negative value = savings in costs, in comparison with option A Positive value = increased revenues or increased costs in comparison with option A					

Figure 3.1: Years of use and financial effects of the three options

- The net present values are based on an internal rate of return of 10%. This not only covers the interest on the capital invested but also includes a risk surcharge.
- Since the defective lathe must in any case be replaced and the required investment of 180,000 francs is covered by insurance, Mr. Mordasini reduces the investment expenditure of options B and C in the calculation by this amount.
- As the illustration shows, both options yield a positive net present value. The net present value of option C is better than the net present value of option B. This is true not only in absolute terms, but also in relation to the amount invested.

Op-tion	Net present value	Revenue/expenditure differences for options B and C compared with option A in years 0 to 8								
		0	1	2	3	4	5	6	7	8
B	-	-180	+40	+40	+40	+40	+40	+40	+40	+40
	+34	-180	+36	+33	+30	+27	+25	+23	+21	+19
C	-	-890	+150	+250	+350	+350	+350	+350	-	-
	+369	-890	+136	+207	+263	+239	+217	+197	-	-

Upper figure   =   Revenue/expenditure differences in thousands of Swiss francs
Lower figure   =   Revenue/expenditure differences in thousands of Swiss francs discounted by the internal rate of return of 10%

Figure 3.2: The net present value calculations for options B and C

On the basis of these calculations, Mr. Mordasini advises the managing director, Mr. Kämpf, to go for option C. Mr. Kämpf accepts this suggestion. Accordingly, Mr. Mordasini gives the order to Kunz, organises the disposal of the old lathe and engages local builders to prepare the foundation and the electrical and water connections for the new machine. He oversees the preparation and installation work, tests and formally accepts the new lathe and checks the relevant invoices.

We have described how a specific decision problem was dealt with. We will now introduce a general descriptive model of a decision-making procedure, which allows a systematization of how decision-making can be approached in practice.

In our descriptive model of a decision-making procedure we must first distinguish between the actor and the decision situation:

- When we talk about the actor, we are referring to the person or group of people, who analyse, evaluate and act. Even though the foreman, Mr. Jäk, the sales manager, Mr. Kessler, the finance director, Mr. Wälti, and the managing director, Mr. Kämpf, were all partially involved in this work, Mr. Mordasini is the actor in this example. As head of production, he takes the urgent measures, analyses the problem, develops problem-solving options and assesses them. He is the de facto decision-maker and organizes its subsequent implementation.
- The decision situation comprises all areas and characteristics of the situation which are relevant to the decision. These will generally include certain parts of the company, specific markets and also the environmental factors relevant to their development. In certain decisions, specific characteristics of the actors can also become part of the decision situation. This is the case, for example, when a manager takes his own abilities and interests into account in the drafting of his job-profile. In our example, the decision situation is the lathe section with its resources, processes and performances. However, the connections between the lathe section and other parts of the company, such as sales, and connections with the outside environment, such as the machine suppliers, are also part of the decision situation.

In addition to the distinction between the actor and the decision situation, typical sub-tasks in decision-making can also be identified:

- The actor receives information about the environment on an ongoing basis. Most of this information is taken in without being subject to any analysis, decisions or actions. However, particular pieces of information like the news of the fire in the lathe in our example, can act as a problem indicator and set a decision-making procedure into motion. From this moment on, the relevant part of the environment is called the decision situation.
- After the discovery of a decision problem analysis normally follows. The actor must understand the problem before he/she can solve it. In the example, the problem is relatively simple to understand and to name. It consists in the replacement of the damaged machine. Mr. Mordasini can therefore concentrate on specifying the basic conditions that the problem solution must fulfill. The results of the analysis form the basis for the development of solution options. In

the example Mr. Mordasini contacts machine manufacturers and asks them to submit offers. Before a decision can be made, the options have to be assessed. In the example, Mr. Mordasini calculates the net present value of options B and C. The analysis, and the subsequent development and assessment of options, cannot take place in a quiet little room; it requires interaction with the decision situation. This is the only way the actor can obtain the information necessary to reach a sound decision. In the example Mr. Mordasini contacts the sales manager, the finance director and the various potential suppliers.

- The better the analysis and the development and assessment of options, the easier it is to take the final decision. In the example, Mr. Mordasini and Mr. Kämpf have no difficulty in choosing option C on the basis of its high net present value.
- After the decision is made, its implementation must be assured. In the example, Mr. Mordasini takes on the ordering of the new lathe as well as coordinating the installation of the new machine.

Figure 3.3 summarises this in graphic form. The result is a model of a decision process. It is a helpful basis on which to analyse and systematize real decision processes. It will also prove useful as a basis for the development of prescriptive suggestions for the solution of decision problems. This is taken up again in Part Two of this book.

3.2   The requirements of a rational decision process

Having developed a descriptive model of a decision-process on the basis of an example, we should now discuss the question of when such a process can be characterized as rational.

We must first distinguish between a substantial or content-based rationality on the one hand and a formal rationality on the other hand (Bamberber & Coenenberg, 2002, p. 3 f.):

- In formal rationality, rationality requirements refer only to the decision process aimed at attaining a given goal. The rationality of the goal itself is not examined.

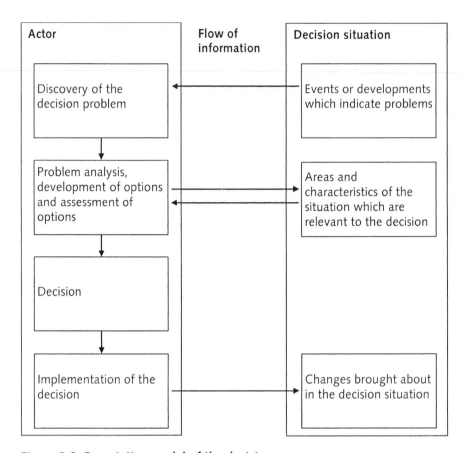

Figure 3.3: Descriptive model of the decision process

- In contrast, substantial or content-based rationality presupposes that the goal must also be examined in terms of its rationality. The goal must be "right"; it is the only justified goal, alongside which all other possible goals appear "wrong". In this case rationality is required not only for the decision process but also for the relevant goal.

Most researchers assume that the choice of goals in decision-making is ultimately a question of subjective values. From a scientific viewpoint, these values cannot be determined to be objectively right or wrong. A large majority view goals in a decision process as pre-determined; the only meaningful basis for the development of decision-making procedures is then the formal rationality of the decision processes themselves. Despite being proponents of formal rationality, we too may consider some goals to be ethically or morally unjustifiable. But where this occurs, it is to be understood as a personal, subjective value judgment and not as a scientific claim.

Those who consider their own goals to be the only correct ones are making the claim that they are in possession of the one and only true theory, from which they can derive these goals, or that their value judgments (for example ideological or religious judgments) are simply superior to the concerns of other people. As scientific researchers, the authors of this book reject such positions. All further deliberations, therefore, will be based on the concept of formal rationality.

So what are the requirements that a decision process must fulfil if it is to be justly called a "formally rational" process?

It is frequently argued that in practice it is eventual success or failure which retrospectively determines what a rational or irrational decision is. But later success or failure is no yardstick. One must distinguish clearly between a rational and a successful decision. While rational action ought to produce more successful decisions, to assume that with formal rationality one could overcome the many uncertainties inherent in a decision and guarantee success would represent a false understanding of rationality. Eisenführ & Weber clarify the difference between successful and rational decisions with the following simple examples: If after careful analysis, you make an investment in shares and your investment later takes a nose dive, the decision does not become less rational because of this. If a student puts down his last hundred euro on number 17 in a roulette game and actually wins, the decision is no more rational because of this success than it would be otherwise (Eisenführ & Weber, 1999, p. 4).

So rationality does not refer to the success or the effective consequences of the chosen option; rather it refers to how thoroughly and systematically the decision process is carried out. In general one assumes that a decision can be described as rational if the decision process exhibits the following characteristics (Kühn, 1969, p. 6 ff.):

(1) The decision process is totally goal-oriented; it consistently focuses on the goal or goals.
(2) The deliberations used in the decision process are based on relevant information which is evaluated as objectively as possible.
(3) The decision process follows a systematic, structured procedure of action and uses clear methodical rules; it is comprehensible to non-participants.

We now comment on each of these in turn.

The goal orientation requirement for formal rational decisions (Characteristic 1) affects all the essential deliberations in the decision process. The very first step, problem discovery, refers to goals which are not being achieved or where performance in achieving them could be improved. Problem analysis is a search for explanations for attaining goals. These explanations help to identify the key decision variables relevant to improved goal attainment. As regards the development of options, only measures that promise a degree of improvement in the fulfilment of the goal should be discussed. Finally, the evaluation of options which is essential for the selection of the best option will be based on decision criteria which have been derived from goals.

The requirement for a decision process to be based on relevant data used as objectively as possible (Characteristic 2) may seem obvious, but requires further examination. Formal rationality does not require information to be complete, totally objective and even certain. "As possible" is important; it allows for the constraints of real decision situations in which financial resources for procuring information are typically very limited. In accordance with the goal-orientation of formal rational decisions, cost-benefit analysis is used before procuring information. The financial importance and the degree of risk a problem presents will determine how much expenditure is justified on information procurement.

We saw in the first chapter that rationality cannot replace intuition and experience and that these faculties may be used in the decision process where appropriate. Formal rationality strives to deliver information which is as objective as possible rather than purely objective information and targets selective information rather than complete information.

A systematic, structured procedure and clear methodical rules (Characteristic 3) lead to deliberations which are understandable to non-participants. The results of such a process should appear well-founded to outsiders. However, the outsiders may be pursuing different objectives and may interpret information differently or indeed have quite different information at their disposal. This can have the effect that they would decide differently than the actor.

3.3   Support for rational decision making from management science

One of the main focuses of management science is to support executives in dealing with decisions. In addition, management science, like all science, also pursues the goal of explaining reality.

Management as science contributes to practice in two ways:
- Empirical analytical management science develops explanatory models. These explanations of reality can be used in decision-making to predict future developments and to determine the effects of options. Models of purchasing behaviour are a typical example of explanatory models. They show marketing managers how buyers perceive the different offers in a market, how they assess them and how they finally decide in favour of a particular offer.
- Practical normative management science proposes decision-making procedures which can help the actor deal with decision problems.

This book belongs in the second category. In Part Two, a procedure for dealing with complex decision problems will be introduced. To make it possible to classify and justify this procedure, Chapter 4 will first explain and illustrate the most important types of decision-making procedures.

4   Decision-making procedures

4.1   Important terms in decision-making

To establish a basis for communication and facilitate the understanding of what follows, some important terms will now be presented.

The decision-maker is often referred to as the *actor*. However, the actor can be one person or a group of individuals. When a number of people have to decide together, it becomes more difficult to make the decision. This is not only because there will be different ideas about how to solve the problem, but above all because there will be different opinions regarding the goals and as a result of this, differing views of what the problem actually is. Part Two of this book is based on the assumption that there is a single actor; problems in collective decision-making are only taken up in Part Three.

As explained in section 2.2, we refer to as a *goal* any state which is desired and striven for by the actor. Since an actor normally pursues more than one goal, a decision is normally oriented towards a *goal system*. Within a goal system it is quite possible that different goals may contradict each other. Moreover the actor cannot always express the goals precisely. A goal system is therefore a complex phenomenon.

Goals are often formulated rather vaguely, so they must be defined in a more specific way before they can be used in decision-making to evaluate the options. The specific formulation of a goal for evaluation of options in a particular decision problem is called a *decision criterion*.

Here are two examples. High product quality may be a goal. If a DIY store wants to offer high quality electric drills, possible decision criteria would be (1) reliability/susceptibility to repair and (2) the number of different functions. In contrast, in a machine factory, the quality of the lathes produced could be measured primarily by the degree of their precision.

An actor typically has more than one starting point from which to approach a decision problem. These may be referred to as *decision variables* or decision dimensions. For example, a manufacturer of plant pots which needs to review its product range might have two decision variables: the number of different products and the materials used in production.

Decisions are not based on single decision dimensions but on combinations of them. **Figure 4.1** gives an example: the producer of plant pots who has to determine the future product range will not decide separately on the number of items and on the materials but will develop and evaluate combinations. The six combinations in Figure 4 are referred to as *options* or alternatives. The two terms are used synonymously.

The alternatives must be formulated so that each alternative excludes all the others. The alternatives presented in Figure 4.1 illustrate this. The totality of all options is called the solution space or option space.

Number of items \ Material	Ceramic only	Ceramic and plastic	Plastic only
50	Option 1	Option 3	Option 5
100	Option 2	Option 4	Option 6

Figure 4.1: Product range options for a producer of plant pots

Everything resulting from the implementation of an option which is relevant for the attainment of the goals is referred to as the *consequences* of the option. By establishing decision criteria, the actor determines which effects of options are significant and are to be considered as consequences. Take for example a decision about where to have a winter holiday; decision criteria might be the probability of good snow conditions, the range of evening entertainment and the overall cost. For each holiday destination option, it is necessary to determine the consequences for each of these three criteria.

Typically each option will have a number of different consequences, according to the different decision criteria. Additionally, for each criterion, more than one value may have to be included for its consequences: this is the case where environmental developments cannot be predicted with certainty. To evaluate an option, all of its various consequences must be summarised in an overall judgement. This summary of the individual consequences is referred to as the *overall consequence*.

No actor can master the decision situation completely. Those elements of the situation which are significant for the decision but which fall outside the actor's control are referred to as *uncontrollable situation variables*. Uncontrollable situation variables will also influence the consequences of each option. Examples of uncontrollable variables are the general economic climate and existing trade structures. There are also variables in a problem situation which can be controlled or influenced. Controllable features have already been introduced as decision variables. Influencable features of the situation will often be useful as decision criteria.

In the same way that values for decision variables are combined into options, values for different uncontrollable situation features can be summarized into *scenarios*. If a Swiss restaurateur is hesitating between buying either a mountain restaurant in a ski station or a restaurant in a town on the plateau, then the potential for earnings of the mountain restaurant option will depend on the snow and the weather. The actor must therefore determine the consequences of the options for different scenarios, perhaps for a good winter, a mediocre winter and a bad winter.

Figure 4.2 summarizes these terms in diagram form.

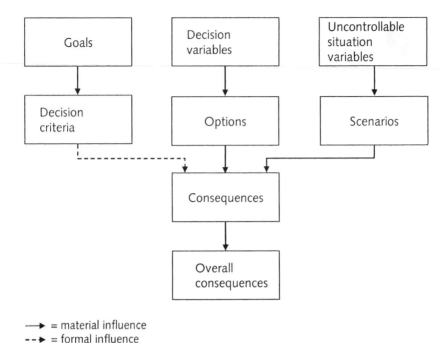

→ = material influence
--▶ = formal influence

Figure 4.2: Central terms in decision methodology and relationships between them

4.2   Decision-making procedure defined

A decision-making procedure can be defined as a system of rules for obtaining and analysing information which can be applied to the reso-lution of a certain type of decision problem (Grünig, 1990, p. 69 f.; Gygi, 1982, p. 20; Klein, 1971, p. 31; Kühn, 1978, p. 52 and 139; Little, 1970, p. B-469 f.; Streim, 1975, p. 145 f.).

A decision-making procedure must present a system of rules which addresses all the essential sub-tasks involved in resolving a decision problem. These are: problem discovery and analysis, the development and evaluation of options, the specification of the overall conse-quences of the options and the decision. Rules that only support the actor in overcoming one of these tasks are not referred to as decision-making procedures. Such rules include techniques to support the search for options, often called creativity techniques, and rules for summarizing individual consequences of an option into its overall consequences, known as decision maxims.

Very different types of rule systems can be found. In form they range from verbal descriptions with or without decision process diagrams to mathematical algorithms of varying degrees of complexity. The content-related differences are more important however. The most important criteria for the differentiation of decision-making procedures and the resultant categories are introduced in section 4.3.

The rules in decision-making procedures refer primarily to the processing of relevant information. They usually only contain vague indications about what information is needed to solve a problem and often make no recommendations as to how to procure the information. This is understandable as the potential for the procurement of decision-relevant information depends on the particular conditions. For this reason it is not possible to make general suggestions for action, beyond recommending how certain empirical research methods may best be used.

4.3   The different types of decision-making procedures

4.3.1   The parameters of decision-making procedures and their values

Management science aims to support the decision-maker in his task and has proposed a large number of procedures. They can be subdivided according to a number of parameters. From a practical viewpoint, three parameters seem important:
- the range of different problems that the procedures can be applied to
- the formal restrictions on the use of the procedures
- the quality of the solutions produced

First we can distinguish between general decision-making procedures, helpful in tackling any problem, and problem-specific ones designed to handle particular types of problem. Two examples of problem specific procedures are portfolio planning, and determining the optimal quantity of stock to be held of a particular product group.

Secondly, the use of a decision-making procedure can involve restrictive conditions. Some of these will be explicitly named. However, there will also be implicit conditions that manifest themselves to the actor as unexpected restrictions or difficulties during the application of the procedure. The most common formal restriction is that the procedure only admits quantitative decision variables and quantitative decision criteria and thus only takes quantitative aspects of the problem into account. For the moment we will distinguish only between procedures with formal application restrictions and those which have no important formal application restrictions.

Thirdly, as regards the quality of the solution produced by the procedures, it makes sense to distinguish between:
- procedures that aim at an optimal solution
- procedures that do not aim at an optimal solution but normally produce a solution which is considered satisfactory by the actor.

Figure 4.3 provides a summary.

4.3.2   Four types of decision-making procedures

In the previous subsection, three parameters were introduced: the content of the problem, formal application conditions and the quality of the solutions. There is a connection between the two parameters "formal application restrictions" and "quality of solutions": restrictive application conditions make it possible to determine an optimal solution. Equally, the abandonment of narrow formal application conditions means that there is no guaranteed solution and that the best solution that can be found will almost always not be the optimal one. The two parameters therefore represent contrasting ways of tackling a problem.

Parameters	Values	
(1) Content of the problem	General decision-making procedures	Problem specific decision-making procedures
(2) Formal application restrictions	Decision-making procedures with formal application restrictions	Decision-making procedures without significant formal application restrictions
(3) Solution quality	Decision-making procedures that aim at optimal solutions	Decision-making procedures that normally aim at satisfactory solutions

Figure 4.3: The parameters of decision-making procedures and associated values

Based on this view, if we combine two parameters of decision-making procedures, we can now present a total of just four types of decision-making procedures, as shown in **Figure 4.4**.

Formal application restrictions and solution quality \ Content of the problem	General use	Only to tackle specific problems
No significant formal application restrictions; normally aim at satisfactory solutions	General heuristic decision-making procedure	Specific heuristic decision-making procedure
Formal application restrictions; aim at optimal solutions	General analytic decision-making procedure	Specific analytic decision-making procedure

Figure 4.4: Four types of decision-making procedures

4.3.3   A comparison of heuristic and analytic decision-making procedures

Before comparing the two types of decision-making procedure, we must first clarify the word "heuristic" used as both adjective and noun.

- The word "heuristic" has its origin in a verb in ancient Greek that can be translated as "to seek" or "to find". Accordingly, the adjective "heuristic" can be understood as "suitable for finding" (Klein 1971, p. 35).
- Feigenbaum and Feldmann consider a heuristic to be a thinking rule, which helps to reduce the effort or cost of finding a solution to complex problems. This advantage of lower cost must be seen against its disadvantage, the lower solution quality of the decisions. Feigenbaum and Feldmann's definition has found general acceptance in business management literature: "A heuristic ... is a rule of thumb, strategy, trick, simplification, or any other kind of device which drastically limits search for solutions in large problem spaces. Heuristics do not guarantee optimal solutions, in fact, they do not guarantee any solution at all; all that can be said for a useful heuristic is that it offers solutions which are good enough most of the time" (Feigenbaum & Feldmann, 1967, p. 6).

The essential advantage of heuristics in comparison to analytic procedures lies in the almost total absence of formal application restrictions and in their relatively low application costs. The disadvantages are the absence of any guarantee of a solution and, where a solution is found, the lack of guarantee that it is the optimal solution. **Figure 4.5** shows the difference between heuristic and analytic decision-making procedures schematically.

As we have seen, analytic decision-making procedures guarantee the optimal solution by having drastic formal application restrictions. If any of the formal requirements for analytic procedures is not fulfilled, the actor will have to resort to a heuristic decision-making procedure. **Inset 4.1** explains the conditions which must be met in the use of analytic procedures and allows us to position heuristic procedures more precisely.

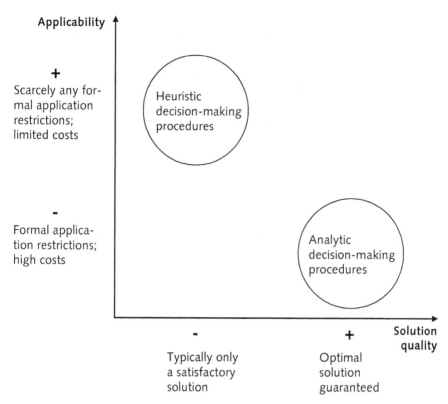

Figure 4.5: Comparison of heuristic and analytic decision-making procedures

---

Inset 4.1: Well-structured problems as a prerequisite for the use of analytic decision-making procedures

According to Simon and Newell (1958, p. 4 ff.), a problem must be "well-structured" before an analytic decision-making procedure can be applied. To qualify as well-structured, the problem must satisfy three specific conditions.

The first condition for the use of an analytic procedure is that the problem contains only quantitative variables or can be described in such a way that it is reduced to quantitative dimensions.

The limitation to quantitative dimensions is not the only require-ment: the second condition is that clear rules must specify whether a given solution is acceptable or not. Where such rules exist, a problem is considered well-defined; if no such rules are available, it is referred to as an ill-defined problem (Klein, 1971, p. 32; Minsky, 1961, p. 408).

Rules of this kind exist for the game of chess. The rules make it unequivocally clear whenever a player's king is in checkmate and thus determine that the opposing player has won. The question of who may be applying the rules is irrelevant since they leave no room for subjective judgments.

But we can still speak of a well-defined problem when the rules for the selection of allowable options include subjective judgments. This is the case, for example, if it is necessary to take into account the actor's attitude to risk when determining whether an option is allowable. In this case the procedure remains independent of the actor; however, the use of the procedure will be based on subjec-tively different attitudes to risk which will influence the assessment of the options.

Even though a problem may be expressed uniquely in quantitative dimensions and may be well-defined, there remains a third condi-tion. It must be possible to develop an analytic procedure which the actor can use without exceeding reasonable limits on time and expenditure (Klein, 1971, p. 32 ff.) Up to now, this has not suc-ceeded for chess, for example: there is no procedure that contains a guarantee of winning a game. If there were such a procedure, the question would certainly arise as to whether it would involve acceptable expenditure. The chess programmes that exist today are based on heuristic rather than analytical rule systems.

According to Simon and Newell, if there is an analytic procedure which can be applied within acceptable time and expenditure limits or if such a procedure can be discovered, then we may speak of a well-structured problem. In all other cases, we will be dealing with an ill-structured problem (Klein, 1971, p. 32; Simon & Newell, 1958, p. 4 ff.)

As **Figure 4.6** shows, a problem must be well structured if an ana-lytic procedure is to be applied. If one of the three conditions for a well-structured problem is not satisfied, only a heuristic decision-making procedure can be used.

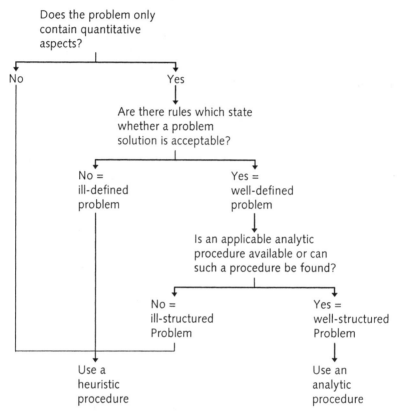

Figure 4.6: The three requirements for using an analytic procedure

4.3.4   Examples of the different types of decision-making procedures

To give the reader a more concrete idea of the different types of decision-making procedures, three examples of procedures are now presented. This will make it possible to clarify the differences between the different types of procedure.

Since Part II provides a full description of a general heuristic decision-making procedure, we can omit an example from this category of procedure for the moment: Chapter 5 gives an overview of this.

As an example of a specific heuristic decision-making procedure, we present the procedure for developing a corporate strategy. Based on portfolio analysis and planning (Hill & Jones, 1992, p. 281 ff.), this procedure is used to set out target market positions and investment priorities for the various businesses of a company diversified geographically and/or in its range of products (Grünig & Kühn, 2005, p. 33 ff.).

The development of corporate strategy follows the five steps shown in **Figure 4.7** (Grünig, 2002, p. 85 ff.; Grünig & Kühn, 2005, p. 195 ff.):

1. The process begins with the definition of the existing businesses. A business is a market offer with its own marketing-mix or at least independence in fixing the most important marketing instruments. When a business shares the market and/or resources with other businesses, we speak of a business unit. However, when a business has only slight market and resource interdependencies with other businesses, we speak of a business field (Grünig & Kühn, 2005, p. 127 ff.). The businesses of a company may be product groups and/or country-based activities.

2. Step Two consists of describing the existing strategy and making a forecast of relevant future developments. To do this, the current portfolio is set up, and future changes in market attractiveness are determined.

3. In the third step, the existing strategy is evaluated, and future strategic options are developed and assessed. First, an evaluation of the situation should be undertaken on the basis of the current portfolio and of predicted changes in market attractiveness. The balance of the portfolio is pivotal for this assessment. A portfolio can be regarded as balanced if it has both businesses with development potential and businesses with a strong current position in mature markets. After assessing the current strategy, options for the future strategy are worked out. At the corporate level, strategic options include the elimination of existing businesses, the reinforcement of existing businesses and the construction of new businesses. This may involve diversification, mergers and acquisitions and strategic

alliances. This step ends with assessment of the options; the option judged best is chosen as the future corporate strategy.

4. In the fourth step, action programmes must be set up to implement the chosen future strategy. In addition, an investment framework must be specified for each of the businesses.

5. Before approving the corporate strategy, it is subjected to a final check. Besides evaluating the consistency of goals and actions, the risks connected with the strategy must be assessed. The capability to finance the strategy also needs to be tested. It sometimes happens that the implementation costs of the strategy exceed the financial means of the company. In this case, the actors must reshape the strategic goals and implementation programmes (and not just the implementation programmes).

Figure 4.8 shows a General Electrics and Mc Kinsey portfolio for the Baer retail group. The portfolio summarizes the current situation and the chosen future corporate strategy. As the figure shows, the Baer group possesses a department store, a number of Body Shops and an

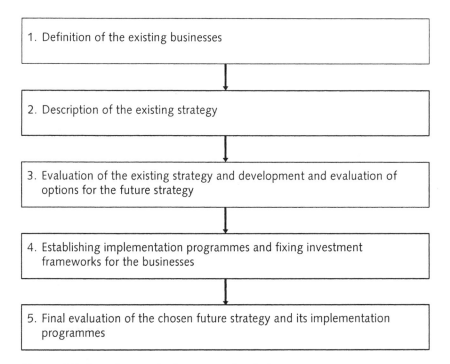

Figure 4.7: Development of a corporate strategy
(adapted from Grünig & Kühn, 2005)

advertising agency. Since the three businesses are relatively independent in terms of markets and resources, they are business fields.
The most important business field, on the basis of turnover and profit,
is the department store; this is separated into different business units.
The portfolio shows the plan: the business field "advertising agency"
and the business unit "food" will be abandoned and the competitive
strength of the business fields "Body Shops" and "Textiles" significantly increased. The other businesses are in markets which are declining in market attractiveness and these businesses will therefore
aim simply at maintaining their current market positions.

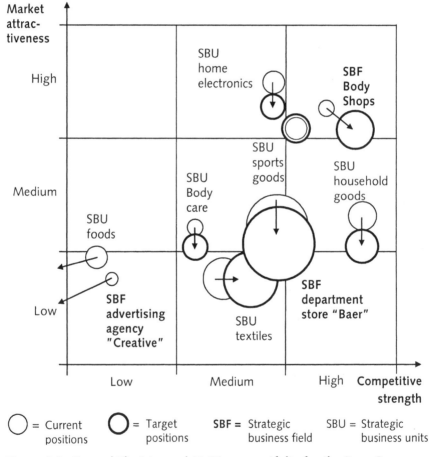

Figure 4.8: General Electrics and McKinsey portfolio for the Baer Group

A good example of a general analytic decision-making procedure is linear programming. The technique is illustrated here with a simple example based on Haberstock (1982, p. 189 ff.). The decision problem contains only two decision variables. This allows us to present the finding of the solution graphically. If more than two decision variables exist - and in practice this will be the norm - the algorithm follows the same procedure in the multi-dimensional decision space.

A company produces and sells two products (I and II) each of which passes through three cost centres (A,B and C). The two products make different use of the capacities available in the cost centres. Each product has maximum sales quantities as well as a pre-determined price.

On the basis of the data shown in **Figure 4.9**, we can determine which product types should be produced in which quantities so that the company maximizes its profit. Neither the available capacities nor the upper sales limits, determined with the help of market research, may be exceeded (Haberstock, 1982, p. 189 ff.)

Product information			
Product	Selling price in USD	Variable costs in USD	Maximum sales
I	40	35	7,500 items/year
II	25	15	4,000 items/year
Cost centre information			
Cost centre	Capacity	Product I processing time	Product II processing time
A	300,000 min./year	30 min./item	50 min./item
B	675,000 min./year	45 min./item	150 min./item
C	280,000 min./year	35 min./item	20 min./item
Fixed costs information			
Annual fixed costs	USD 35,000		

Figure 4.9: Data for determining optimal sales and production programmes (adapted from Haberstock, 1982, p.190)

The information from Figure 4.9 is now incorporated step-by-step into **Figure 4.10**. Its horizontal axis indicates the number of items for product I and its vertical axis the number of items for product II:

- First, the two restrictions on sales and the three production restrictions are entered.
- Next, the option space is determined.
- After this the gradient for the goal function is determined. Since twice the contribution margin can be achieved with one item of product II compared to one item of product I, twice as many items of product I are needed to attain the same contribution margin. Therefore the goal function is relatively flat.
- The line representing the goal function is now moved up parallel as far as it will go without leaving the option space.

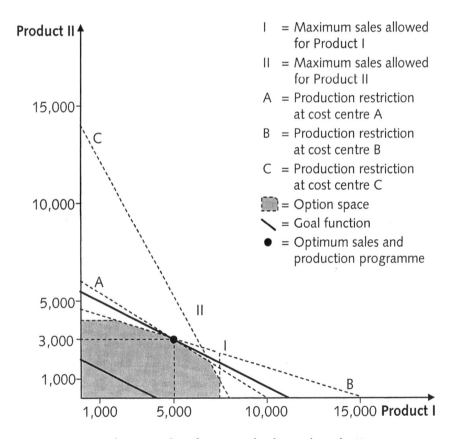

Figure 4.10: Graphic procedure for optimal sales and production programmes

- As can be seen in the figure, the optimum sales and production programme is 5,000 items of product I and 3,000 items of product II. The maximum achievable profit amounts to USD 20,000. This is calculated as follows: 5,000 items x USD 5 + 3,000 items x USD 10 - USD 35,000.

Harris and Wilson's model for determining the optimal order quantity for a commodity offers an example of a specific analytic decision-making procedure (Popp, 1968). As shown in **Figure 4.11**, the model assumes both a constant demand for the items of the commodity and delivery of all quantities ordered without any time delay. Further, it is assumed that the order quantity has no influence on the procurement price and that sufficient storage space exists for any quantity, so that there are never extra rental expenses for storage space. Based on all these assumptions, the model is able to minimize costs dependent on order quantity. Costs dependent on order quantity are of two kinds. First, there are expenses accrued with each order process. These will be proportionately higher when smaller quantities are ordered. Second, there are storage costs, which will be higher for larger quantities.

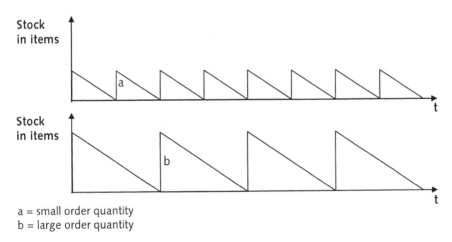

a = small order quantity
b = large order quantity

Figure 4.11: Harris and Wilson's saw-tooth model of stock movements

Figure 4.12 shows the two cost components, the total costs and the minimum total costs, calculated using the Harris and Wilson model. Mathematically, the figure for the minimum costs is determined as follows: first derivation of the total cost function is set at zero. Then the value of Q in this equation is calculated.

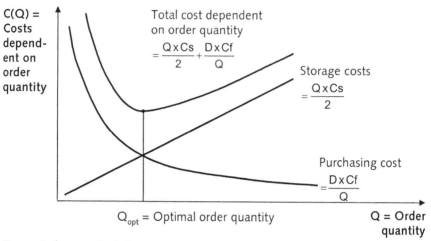

Q = Order quantity in items.
$C(Q)$ = Cost dependent on order quantity
D = Annual demand in items
Cf = Fixed cost per order
Cs = Storage costs per item and year

Figure 4.12: Costs dependent on order quantity and minimum costs in the Harris-Wilson model

The three examples give us an opportunity to clarify the differences between the four types of decision-making procedures once again:

- The procedure for developing a corporate strategy and the Harris-Wilson model for determining the optimal order quantity are suitable for dealing with a specific type of problem. The name of the decision-making procedure itself indicates the type of problem. These two procedures are therefore specific decision-making procedures. In contrast, linear programming is suitable for the optimization of any well-structured problem: it can determine the optimal investment programme of a company, solve a transportation problem or - as in the example - determine the optimal sales and production programme for a given period of time. Linear programming therefore belongs in the category of general decision-making procedures.

- Both Harris and Wilson's procedure and linear programming have very restrictive formal requirements for use: the quantitative information which must be provided is very precisely fixed. If one piece of this information is missing, the decision-making procedure can not be applied or its use will produce a de facto sub-optimal and potentially even absurd result. If one piece of the quantitative information is wrong, the procedure will produce a calculation which is correct on paper but which is not correct in reality. Both of these procedures can be classified as analytic decision-making procedures. In contrast to these, the procedure for developing a corporate strategy requires no precise quantitative information. If the actor has such information, this will increase the quality of the solution, but it is not absolutely necessary for applying the procedure. Whatever the information available, this decision-making procedure is unable to produce the optimal solution and it will be impossible to estimate how far the developed strategy may be from the optimum. As this discussion shows, the procedure for developing a corporate strategy falls into the class of heuristic decision-making procedures.

Part Two: A general heuristic decision-making procedure

Part Two presents our recommended decision-making procedure and explains how to use it. After working through Part Two:

- You will be familiar with a possible approach to tackling complex decision problems.
- You will know how to go about each of the steps in the procedure.

As a result you will be able to work systematically through any complex decision problem you may encounter and to find a satisfactory solution to it.

Part Two has five chapters:

- Chapter Five gives an overview of the whole procedure and explains its basis and its use.
- Chapter Six explains Step One: "Discovering the decision problem" and Step Two "Analysing the decision problem". Approaches to the systematic discovery of problems were already presented in Chapter Two. Here we add a discussion of what is known as ad hoc problem discovery and we treat the assessment of problem relevance. The main part of the chapter examines in detail each of the various steps within problem analysis and naming.
- Chapter Seven moves on to consider the search for options and their assessment. These issues arise in Steps Three to Six of the decision-making procedure. The chapter deals with each step in turn, beginning with the development of options. After this comes the question of criteria for their assessment. We recognise that there may be variables in the problem situation which cannot be controlled and we therefore next consider the question of how to deal with this uncertainty. The results of Steps Three, Four and Five allow the setting up of a decision matrix and this matrix will then structure the work of Step Six: the determination of the consequences of the options.
- Chapter Eight looks at the decision itself. The chapter begins by distinguishing between problems for which an intuitive decision may be made and those which require the determination of the total consequences of the options with the help of decision maxims. Afterwards, an overview of decision maxims is presented, together

with an indication of when each maxim can be used. Then the maxims are explained in detail. The chapter closes with an assessment of these decision maxims.

- Chapter Nine provides an extended example of the application of the decision-making procedure. After an introduction to the case, we see how the problem is discovered, analysed and named. Next comes the development and assessment of options and the chapter closes with the presentation and justification of the decision.

5   Overview of the decision-making procedure

5.1   The value of a general heuristic decision-making procedure

Before we come to an overview, we first examine the advantages and limitations of a general heuristic decision-making procedure. It is important that, from the very beginning, readers and potential users of the procedure should approach it with realistic expectations.

There are two ways in which we can judge the value of a general heuristic decision-making procedure:

- It may be assessed in relation to decisions made intuitively, without using a formal procedure.
- It may be assessed in relation to decisions reached by using a specific heuristic procedure.

In what follows we will consider each of these comparisons.

First of all, it is clear that in both systematic and intuitive procedures the question remains open as to whether the correct goals are pursued. As we have seen, it is always a matter of subjective assessment to determine whether a particular goal is to be considered valid. Secondly, both approaches, intuitive and procedurally-based, have in common the fact that the quality of the decision finally made will depend at least to some extent on the actor's knowledge of the facts. The option retained will usually represent a considerably better decision if the actor has a sufficiency of information about the problem than if the opposite is the case. However there remain at least three clear advantages of a systematic procedure over an intuitive one:

- Using a procedure makes it easier to focus all the various tasks in the decision process on the overall objective. It thus reduces the chance that wrong decisions will come about as a result of losing sight of the objectives during the process.
- By differentiating between analysis, the development of options and the assessment of these options, a procedure makes it easier to distinguish clearly between factual knowledge and subjective assessment. This produces transparency in the decision-making.
- The systematic approach inherent in a procedure allows for a better use of the available knowledge base. This typically produces not

only better quality decisions, but also a more efficient decision-making process. Efficiency is increased because errors in thinking and contradictions are uncovered much more rapidly.

When we compare the general heuristic decision-making procedure with a specific heuristic decision-making procedure, the judgment we make will depend on how far the particular decision problem matches the type of problem that the specific procedure is designed to deal with. Where the match is a very good one, the specific decision-making procedure will normally lead to a better result. This is because the steps in the process and the questions addressed in those steps are finely tuned to the problem type and allow the actor to make better use of his knowledge base. However, the more the essential features of a given problem deviate from the features of the problem-type that the specific procedure was designed to handle, the more likely it is that the use of the specific procedure is less effective than the use of the general procedure. In this case the use of the specific procedure will only produce a good solution for a sub-problem, or worse, will lead to the solution of an irrelevant problem.

At this point we would like to stress once again that wrong decisions always remain possible; the quality of a decision will always depend to a large extent on the capabilities and knowledge of the actor.

Figure 5.1 summarizes the advantages and limitations of a general decision-making procedure.

5.2   The proposed sequence of tasks

Figure 5.2 shows the various tasks of the basic form of our decision-making procedure. For complex decision problems problem analysis usually produces a number of sub-problems. **Figure 5.3** illustrates the application of the procedure in this case. As an illustration, it shows the course of action for solving two sub-problems, either in parallel or one after the other.

Advantages	Limitations
Can be used for all decision problems	Less effective and efficient for special types of decision problem than special procedures, where these are available and practicable
Increases the focus on the objectives and thus lessens the risk of wrong decisions	Cannot guarantee that a wrong decision will not be made
Improves the quality of decisions by differentiating between factual knowledge and subjective assessment and by improved use of the knowledge base	Cannot compensate for lack of knowledge or for limited skills of an actor in assessing factual knowledge

Figure 5.1: Advantages and limitations of a general heuristic decision-making procedure

The following points apply to both of these figures:

- Procedural tasks are differentiated from substantive tasks. Procedural tasks devote time to planning how to overcome the problem; timing and personnel decisions have to be made and communicated to those concerned. In the procedural steps, the decision problem is not processed. However, careful deliberation at the procedural level increases the speed and the efficiency of the subsequent treatment of the substantive problems.
- As Figure 5.2 illustrates, Steps 3 to 7 can be gone through several times. This is necessary if the overall assessment of the options has yielded no satisfactory result and the problem must therefore be processed further. This loop is likely to occur if the Generate and Test heuristic (see Inset 5.1) is applied. In this case only one option at a time is developed and assessed. This process is repeated until an acceptable solution is found.
- If the problem analysis yields two separate sub-problems, they can be processed in parallel, as shown on the left side of Figure 5.3. As complete independence only occurs in exceptional cases, the deci-

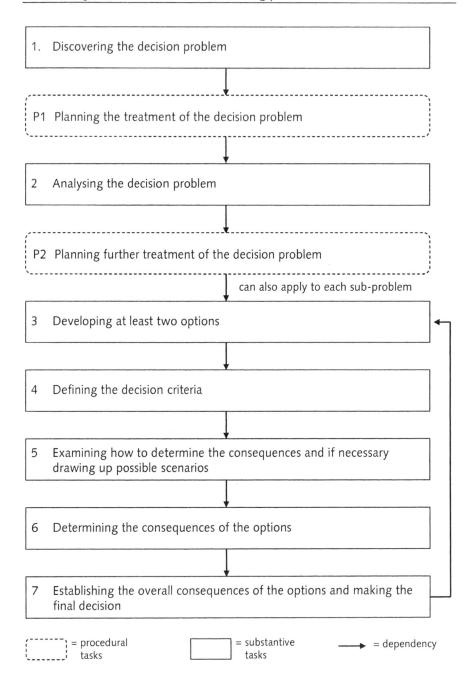

Figure 5.2: The general heuristic decision-making procedure in the basic form

sions on the two sub-problems must be coordinated. The right side of Figure 5.3 shows a situation where the problem analysis yields a hierarchy of two sub-problems. In this situation, the superordinate problem is processed first. The option chosen for this sub-problem forms the basis for the treatment of the subordinate sub-problems. Obviously other, more complex cases are also possible. For example, the problem analysis can yield a sub-problem "A" parallel to two other sub-problems "B1" and "B2" which are themselves in a hierarchical relationship.

- Figure 5.2 and Figure 5.3 show only one heuristic loop leading back from Step 7 to Step 3. This is the most important feedback loop. It is inherent in heuristic processes, however, that loops can occur at all stages in the procedure. For example, it is possible that decision criteria determined in Step 4 must be revised because Step 6 shows that the options cannot be assessed. Another example of a possible loop is shown on the right side of Figure 5.3: in the case of two successive sub-problems, it is possible that no satisfactory solution can be found for the subordinate sub-problem. Here one must re-examine the options for the subordinate sub-problem. To keep the diagram clear, the many other possible loops have not been included.

5.3   A brief explanation of the tasks

In section 5.2 the structure of the general decision-making procedure was introduced. We will now explain the seven substantive steps and the two procedural steps in this procedure. The reader will be given an overview of the tasks that must be carried out when applying the procedure.

In **Step 1**, the actor can identify a decision problem in one of two different ways:
- The first possibility is that a divergence is discovered ad hoc between the current situation and the target situation. The actor is likely to have a vague rather than a precise idea of the target situation and goals. As knowledge of the current situation, too, is never

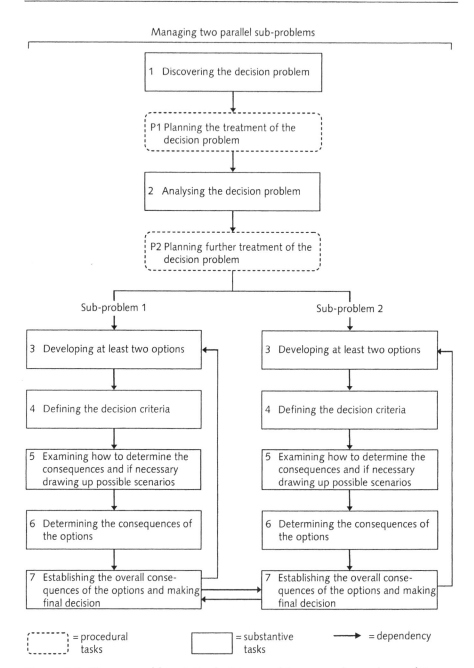

Figure 5.3: The general heuristic decision-making procedure when solving parallel or consecutive sub-problems

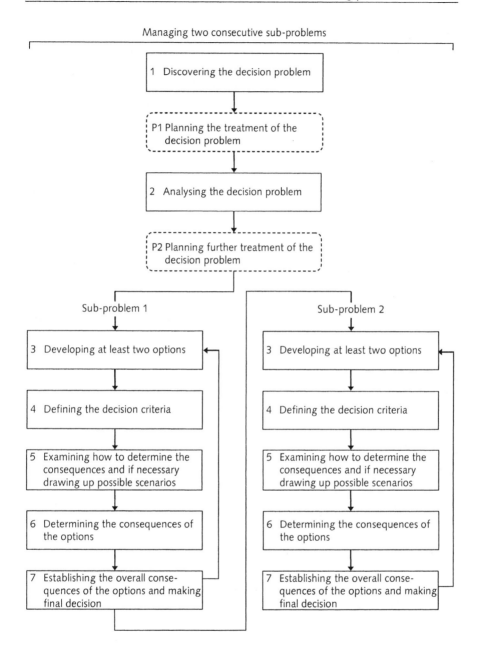

Managing two consecutive sub-problems

1 Discovering the decision problem

P1 Planning the treatment of the
    decision problem

2 Analysing the decision problem

P2 Planning further treatment of the
    decision problem

Sub-problem 1

3 Developing at least two options

4 Defining the decision criteria

5 Examining how to determine the
   consequences and if necessary
   drawing up possible scenarios

6 Determining the consequences of
   the options

7 Establishing the overall consequences of the options and making
   final decision

Sub-problem 2

3 Developing at least two options

4 Defining the decision criteria

5 Examining how to determine the
   consequences and if necessary
   drawing up possible scenarios

6 Determining the consequences of
   the options

7 Establishing the overall consequences of the options and making
   final decision

complete and precise, it logically follows that one can only have a vague idea about the difference. Accordingly, we should only speak of a decision problem if this difference between current and target situations fulfils two conditions: firstly it has to be significant, and secondly there must be a strong probability that it is not a false alarm but that the problem really exists.

- Problem-finding systems can help to identify problems. These systems provide values for certain environmental and business variables, known in decision methodology as problem indicators. The values are determined either continuously or at regular intervals. When these indicators exceed or fall short of certain predefined limits then a decision problem exists.

Once a problem has been identified, whether ad hoc or with the help of a problem-finding system, the person or team dealing with it must first make clear in procedural **Step P1** who is to have the task of processing the problem and in what time frame. The amount of time and energy devoted to the analysis and solution of the problem depends on the perceived importance and urgency of the case. Because only the subsequent problem analysis provides reliable assessment of these two aspects, in this step it must be assumed that the problem has relatively high importance and urgency.

After dealing with the organizational and timing aspects, the real problem-solving begins with problem analysis in **Step 2**. This step is almost always the most time-consuming, and frequently also the most difficult. But it is crucial for the quality of the problem solution. The following principles should be valid for all types of problem. However, as each problem is unique, they are quite abstract:

- The starting point of problem analysis is the identified problem. The end point of problem analysis is either a single named problem or a number of named parallel or consecutive problems.
- Problem analysis begins with an overview of the starting position. The most important facts are collected and connections between them examined. Then the possible problem causes are determined. The path to be chosen for this is working backward: **Figure 5.4** illustrates schematically how it works. Starting with all the various factors considered possible causes at the time of the discovery of the problem, step by step different possible causes are discarded.

Once the problem causes have been more or less specifically identified, the actor must name the problem or the sub-problems and decide on the dependency relationships between the sub-problems.
- Good problem analysis means the careful investigation of facts and their evaluation through structured, logical reasoning. In practice this has a lot to do with common sense. However models are also helpful; they display the links between different relevant variables within the situation and this can help to understand and structure the problem.

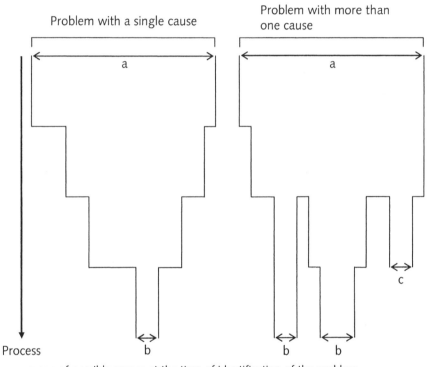

Problem with a single cause

Problem with more than one cause

Process

a = range of possible causes at the time of identification of the problem
b = specific named problem(s)
c = initially proposed as a problem, but shown not to be a problem by later analysis

Figure 5.4: Backward-moving analysis

Based on the problem analysis, in procedural **Step P2**, it becomes possible to determine what the further treatment of the problem should be:

- Problem analysis shows the importance and urgency of the problem(s) and therefore allows us to plan the timing for overcoming the problem. Where there is more than one problem, the actor can solve these one after the other and/or in parallel. Apart from the importance and urgency of the problem, dependencies among the sub-problems determined in the analysis will play a role in deciding this question.
- Clear problem naming makes it easier to assemble one or more teams with the relevant know-how.

Step 3 in the decision-process consists in working out at least two options to solve the problem. The following principles apply here:

- If it is not possible to develop two fundamentally different options, no real decision problem exists. The problem solving process can be brought to an end and the only practicable solution can be chosen. However, actors should in this case consider carefully whether all the starting points for possible options have been examined. It should also be remembered that the continuation of the status quo is an option in many cases.
- If the continuation of the status quo is a realistic option, the task within Step 3 is reduced to finding at least one additional option.
- From a practical point of view, it seems important that the solution options should make use of the different decision variables and cover the area for possible solutions as well as possible. If a particular solution approach is adopted too quickly the solution space is not covered fully and the optimal option can be in the area not under examination. The result is that the solution finally chosen will be far from the optimum. **Figure 5.5** presents this scenario.

In **Step 4**, the actor has to determine the decision criteria against which the problem solution options should be evaluated. In contrast to the objectives, which are usually a rather vague characterization of the target situation, these decision criteria should be specific and allow the assessment of the options:

- This need for assessment measures which allow us to evaluate the options effectively means that the decision criteria are only defined once the possible solution options are known. Only if the options are known can criteria be identified which are practical and which

Good coverage of the
solution space with options

Poor coverage of the
solution space with options

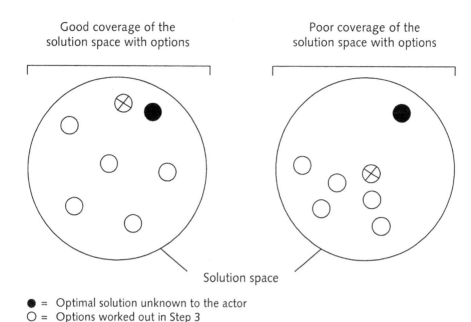

Solution space

● = Optimal solution unknown to the actor
○ = Options worked out in Step 3
⊗ = Solution chosen in Step 7

Figure 5.5: Solution space, solution options and optimal solution

give a ranking of the options in terms of their contributions to the
goals.
- It is possible that a single decision criterion will suffice in order to
assess the options. This case is referred to as a univalent decision
problem. The usual case, however, is that it is only possible to make
a goal-related judgment of the options on the basis of a range of
decision criteria. This is called a polyvalent decision problem.

After suitable decision criteria have been determined in Step 4, **Step 5**
consists in the preparation of the evaluation of the options. The actor
has to give serious thought to the question of whether the effects of
the options are more or less certain, or whether they must be evaluated in parallel for different scenarios. If the consequences are to be
determined simultaneously for several scenarios, these scenarios have
to be established. Wherever possible, probabilities should be allocated. Step 5 can produce three possible results:
- A certain decision.
- A number of different scenarios are identified. For each a probabil-

ity can be attributed. This case produces a decision subject to risk.
- A number of different scenarios are identified, but probabilities cannot be established for them. In this case the decision is referred to as an uncertain decision.

In Step 4 we distinguished between univalent and polyvalent decision problems. In Step 5 we classified decision problems as certain, risk and uncertain. Combining these categories gives us six different decision types. They are significant when identifying the consequences and especially when determining the overall consequences of the options. **Figure 5.6** illustrates these six cases.

	Univalent decision	Polyvalent decision
Certain decision	Certain and univalent decision	Certain and polyvalent decision
Risk decision	Risk and univalent decision	Risk and polyvalent decision
Uncertain decision	Uncertain and univalent decision	Uncertain and polyvalent decision

Figure 5.6: The six decision types

Once the decision problem has been set up in Steps 3 to 5, **Step 6** requires the establishing of the consequence values for each option, for each decision criterion and for each environmental scenario. This task requires knowledge of facts relevant to the problem and the ability to produce forecasts. There are some general statements that can be made in this regard:
- The consequence values can be based on empirical measurements or on subjective assessments. The first approach is obviously preferable. However, since the consequence values very often comprise qualitative aspects, empirically verified consequence values may be the exception.
- The quality of subjective evaluations can be improved by integrating experts in the process: The individuals concerned first establish

the consequences, working separately. Afterwards, they discuss the differences between their assessments and agree on a common solution. This process is similar to a Delphi Study but less costly. Because the individual evaluations are subject to a learning effect with possible changes of opinion, the group judgment is, in general, qualitatively better than the average of the different individual judgments.

In **Step 7** the single consequence values of the options are finally combined to determine the overall consequences and to make the decision:

- In certain and univalent decisions the consequences determined in Step 6 and the overall consequences of the options are identical. In all other decision types, a total judgment of the options must be generated. This can be done either intuitively or analytically. If the actor decides in favour of the analytic approach, rules are needed. These are known as decision maxims. What the maxims must achieve depends on the type of decision problem. There are decision maxims to overcome polyvalence, risk and uncertainty. If you are working on a polyvalent risk problem or on a polyvalent uncertain problem, both a maxim to overcome the polyvalence and another maxim to overcome the risk or the uncertainty will be needed.
- When the overall consequences have been established, the actor can choose one of the options or can go back to Step 3 and work out further options. This loop, shown in Figure 5.2, is required when all the options fail to meet the demands but, at the same time, the hope remains that a better solution can be found.

5.4   The basis of the general heuristic decision-making procedure

Sections 5.2 and 5.3 offered an overview of the procedure. The basis of the procedure is examined in this section.

As can be seen in **Figure 5.7**, the general heuristic decision-making procedure is partly based on contributions from the relevant literature and partly on the experience of the authors.

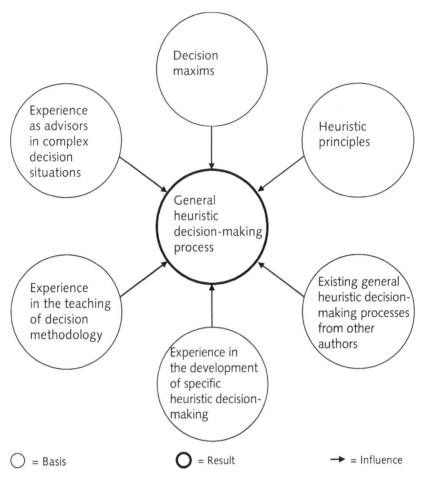

Figure 5.7: The basis of the general heuristic decision-making procedure

The following categories of contributions come from the literature:

- A first important basis is the proposed decision maxims from decision logic literature (see Inset 1.1). These are used in Step 7 for the
  overall assessment of the solution options. They are explained in
  detail in Chapter 8.
- The relevant literature has established heuristic principles which
  must be taken into account in the design of heuristic decision procedures. Inset 5.1 presents the heuristic principles central to the decision-making procedure and shows how they have been respected
  within the procedure.
- Other general heuristic procedures exist in the literature. Compar-

ing our ideas with the suggestions in the literature can help to identify weaknesses and improve our procedure.

There are three particular types of experience which the authors have found especially useful in the development of the procedure proposed here:

- Both individually, and working together, the authors have designed a number of specific heuristic decision-making procedures. In doing so, they learnt a great deal about the particular issue. But above all, this work has developed their knowledge of problem-solving methodology and these insights have been incorporated in the design of the general heuristic decision-making procedure proposed in this book.
- Their teaching of general decision methodology has also produced valuable findings. The methodological recommendations were tested and improved.
- Most valuable of all have been the authors' experiences as consultants to organizations facing complex decision situations. Here too, methods were applied and tested. What seems even more important is the knowledge we have gained about the human situation when top executives face difficult decisions. They have to solve a problem with full use of their intellectual faculties, but at the same time they will usually be under enormous pressure to succeed. In addition, important decisions must often be made at short notice. This experience has been taken into account in the design of the proposed general decision-making procedure.

Inset 5.1: Important heuristic principles and their application in the proposed general heuristic decision-making procedure

Heuristic principles are rules of thumb applied by problem solvers to render complex problems solvable. The most important basic heuristic principles for the proposed decision-making procedure will be explained here. We will also show where they are applied in the procedure. This account is based on Kühn (1978, p. 129 ff.).

The most important heuristic rule used in our procedure is *problem factorisation*. This means that the original, overly complex problem is disassembled into a series of manageable sub-problems. These may represent a sequence or be arranged as parallel problems. The proposed decision-making procedure uses this principle in two ways. On the one hand, the procedure presents a sequence of two procedural and seven substantive component steps, to be completed one after the other. On the other hand from Step 3 onwards a number of the sub-problems can be processed in parallel.

Alongside factorisation the principle of *modelling* is employed. This principle means that the sub-problems distinguished with the help of factorisation should wherever possible be given boundaries, or be "modelled", so that proven problem solving methods can be used. This heuristic principle underlies Step 7: there are a number of decision maxims with whose help the overall consequences of the options can be established and the problem of Step 7 can be solved.

Another important principle is that of *subgoal-reduction*. It proposes that a complex goal or goal system can be attained by completing a series of (relevant) simpler goals. This principle is followed in Step 4 of the suggested procedure: the actor is asked in this step to choose criteria which represent the original goal-system and at the same time allow the options to be assessed.

The heuristic principle of *generate-and-test* demands that new solution options be worked out until a satisfactory solution is found or until the actor must assume that no better solution can be identified. In the decision-making procedure, this principle is applied in the heuristic loop from Step 7 to Step 3: if the overall consequences of the options yield an unsatisfactory result for all evaluated options, further solutions should be sought and assessed. One only gives up once it is clear that no better solution can be found.

A fifth principle underlying all heuristic decision-making procedures is that of Simon's *bounded rationality* (1966, p. 19). It suggests that a satisfactory solution should be sought rather than the optimal solution. In accordance with this, the actor is asked to define a target level, and the generate-and-test process is broken off as soon as a solution reaches this target level. In our procedure, the heuristic principle of bounded rationality is applied in Step 7: after an overall evaluation of the options, the actor must define his/her target level. Afterwards the actor can judge whether to settle for the best of the options or to continue to search for a better solution. Of course the target level is not set in stone. If an intensive search reveals that the level cannot be reached, the actor will be forced to review it. On the other hand, if a number of options worked out in the first round exceed the target, the actor may raise the barrier for an acceptable solution.

6 Discovering and analysing the decision problem

6.1 Discovering the decision problem

The starting point for a conscious decision-making process is a decision problem. More precisely, this means that it is assumed that a situation exists where the overriding goals are not being reached (threat problem), or where performance could be improved (opportunity problem). Thus the term "decision problem" is viewed neutrally, including both threat and opportunity problems. A decision problem is a situation which sets a decision process in motion.

Decision problems can be identified ad hoc or with the help of problem-finding systems. What a problem-finding system is and what types of systems there are is covered in section 2.3 above. Ad hoc problem discovery takes place on the basis of more or less accidental observations "from the situation", so there is little to be said which would be universally valid. We can only point out that:

- The education and experience of executives is important: the better a manager is trained and the more experience he/she has, the sooner he/she will discover problems, whether in meetings and conversations, by examining written records or in the course of personal visits.
- The discovery of problems ad hoc also depends critically on executives being open to the evidence. Conversations, records, and visits will only reveal threats, opportunities and associated decision problems to those who are ready to find them.

As **Figure 6.1** shows, the discovery of the problem is the first step in the general heuristic decision-making procedure. From a strictly logical point of view, the discovery of the problem cannot be a step in the problem-solving procedure: before it can be analysed and then solved with the help of a procedure, the decision problem first has to be discovered. But for obvious reasons, it is sensible to check thoroughly whether an important decision problem exists before investing time, energy and money in solving the problem. This step is the checking and validation of the problem discovery, which follows on from the

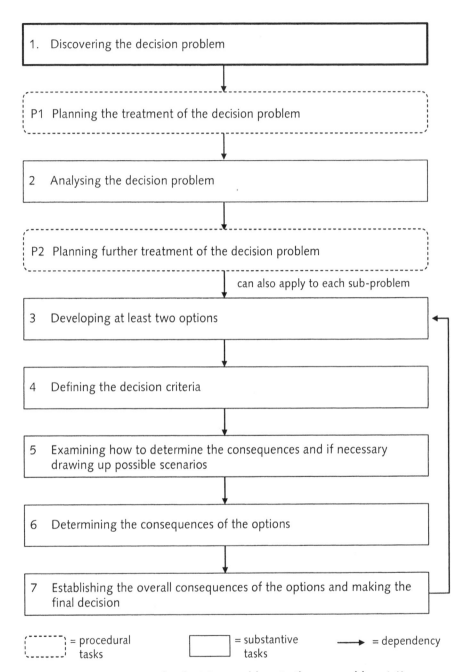

Figure 6.1: Discovering the decision problem in the general heuristic decision-making procedure

problem discovery itself. It would be more precise but more complicated to name this step "validation of the problem discovery".

Before beginning work on solving the problem, the following three questions should be addressed in order to validate the problem:

1. Is there genuinely a considerable difference between the current situation and the target situation? Is there a substantial threat or opportunity?
2. Is the information reliable, on the basis of which the difference between the current and the target situations has been identified and evaluated as important? Can a false alarm be excluded?
3. Is it worth subjecting the problem to a formal decision-making process?

Where problem discovery is based on a problem-finding system using goal-indicators, Question 1 can be answered without much difficulty. Actors who regularly employ goal indicators will usually know what values represent normal variation and what values show a significant problem. **Figure 6.2** illustrates the use of the goal indicator "accumulated product turnover" to determine the presence of a problem. A problem is present when a real indicator value is outside the tolerated range of values.

In many other cases it will be more difficult to answer this first question. This is especially so where the discovery of the problem is ad hoc and where it is an opportunity problem. In such cases, the target and even the current situation can typically only be described in vague terms. What this means is that it will be difficult to assess whether the distance between the two imprecisely described points is in fact of significance. Let us say that one objective of a company is to create attractive jobs. This is a vague target. But assessing the attractiveness of existing jobs may also be difficult, and even if values for the current situation and the target are available, the question remains whether the difference between the two is significant.

The second question to address concerns the reliability of available information about the current situation. If the actor has not obtained the information personally and therefore cannot judge its quality, a

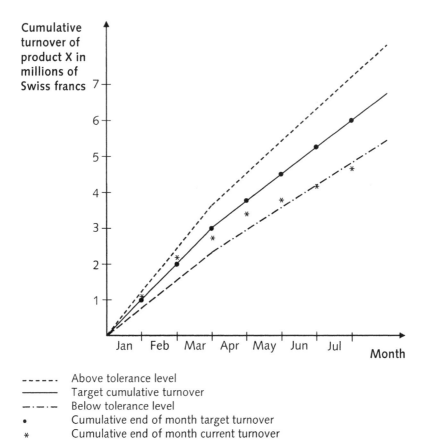

Cumulative
turnover of
product X in
millions of
Swiss francs

Month

------   Above tolerance level
———   Target cumulative turnover
—·—·—   Below tolerance level
•   Cumulative end of month target turnover
*   Cumulative end of month current turnover

Figure 6.2: Problem discovery on the basis of a goal indicator

check is recommended. For example, how was job attractiveness determined? Is the value for the current situation based on a survey
using a representative sample? Were the most important dimensions
of job attractiveness included in the survey? Could the employees
participating in the survey make their statements without fear of reac-
tions from superiors or colleagues? We should only speak of a problem once the current situation has been stated with a reasonable degree of reliability and completeness.

The third question asks whether the significant discrepancy between
current and target situation is a problem which requires systematic
treatment. As a general principle, it is worth analysing the discrepancy
and trying to eliminate or reduce it, if the costs involved in doing this

are smaller than the benefits it will bring. However, as neither cost nor benefits can be stated precisely at this stage of validation of the problem, the third question can only be answered summarily. Despite this, before setting up a team to analyse the problem, it is undoubtedly a sound move to spend some time estimating the costs of this, together with the expected return.

6.2   Analysing the decision problem

6.2.1   General considerations for problem analysis and naming

As can be seen in **Figure 6.3**, problem analysis is the second component in the general heuristic decision-making procedure. The outcome of Step 2 requires that the problem discovered in Step 1 should be well understood so that targeted solution options can then be developed in Step 3. Although this task may not appear very exciting, it often represents the most important and the most difficult step in the whole decision-making procedure:

- A good understanding of the problem is important, because otherwise the options developed in Step 3 may focus on the wrong area or take the wrong approach. Sometimes such mistakes are discovered and corrected during the subsequent option evaluation phase. In this case, all that has been lost is the unnecessary work done. But if the mistake is not discovered then the actor will end up choosing the best solution to a non-existent or unimportant problem. Meanwhile the important problem remains unsolved.
- Problem analysis is difficult because each decision problem has a different structure. This means that it is not possible to provide methodological support which is both universal and specific. Since only relatively abstract methodical recommendations can be offered, for the most part the actor has to rely on himself/herself.

Step 2 is thus typically a complex task, often time-consuming and expensive. It is therefore worth applying the heuristic of factorisation, and breaking it down into sub-tasks. **Figure 6.4** distinguishes four sub-steps, which are each described below.

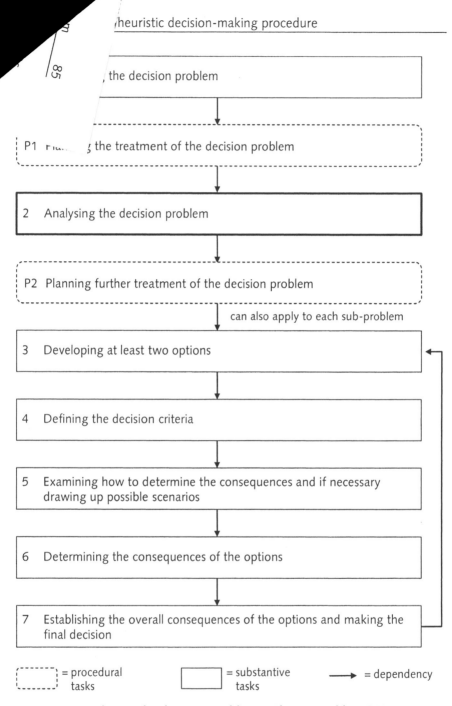

the decision problem

P1 rι.   ξ the treatment of the decision problem

2   Analysing the decision problem

P2 Planning further treatment of the decision problem

can also apply to each sub-problem

3   Developing at least two options

4   Defining the decision criteria

5   Examining how to determine the consequences and if necessary
     drawing up possible scenarios

6   Determining the consequences of the options

7   Establishing the overall consequences of the options and making the
     final decision

‑‑‑‑‑‑ = procedural
         tasks

☐ = substantive
      tasks

⟶ = dependency

**Figure 6.3: Analysing the decision problem in the general heuristic
decision-making procedure**

It should be noted that the importance of these sub-steps and the resources necessary for their implementation can vary. There are decision problems where problem naming (Sub-step 2.3) and the determining of the problem structure (Sub-step 2.4) are possible without substantial preliminary groundwork, for example, when the chief executive retires and it is clear that a replacement must be found by a certain date. But apart from such exceptional cases, it should be assumed that all four sub-steps of problem analysis will be relevant.

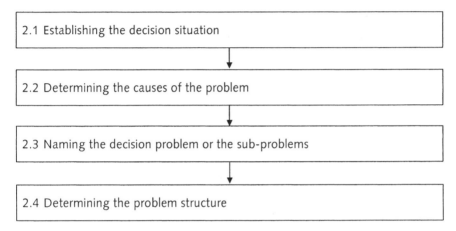

Figure 6.4: Sub-steps in Step 2

6.2.2 Establishing the decision situation

Problem analysis and naming begins with the establishing of the current situation. It makes no sense to begin exploring problem causes until an unambiguous picture of the starting point is available.

Based on the great variety of decision problems, Sub-step 2.1 may comprise very diverse tasks but normally the sub-step includes at least the following three tasks:
- Definition of the area(s) for analysis
- Structured recording of the decision situation
- Forecast of the future development of the decision situation

It is always worth beginning Sub-step 2.1 by carefully defining the area(s) for analysis. Areas for analysis may be organisational units (from individual positions to the company as a whole), business processes and function areas (such as procurement, product development, financing), markets (specific sales or procurement markets) or environmental factors. If the problem is a significant one and it is difficult to localize possible causes, then it is better to broaden the analysis so as not to overlook any important aspects of the problem.

The next task is to record the decision situation in a structured way. If there are different areas of analysis, this is done for each area. What the structured record of the decision situation means exactly and how much work is involved will depend on the particular problem:

- Frequently, a chronology of the previous events is produced and the available documents are arranged accordingly. **Figure 6.5** shows a practical grid for this. For example, if a personnel manager is confronted with a conflict between an employee and his/her direct superior, the manager must try to record the different individual events which have taken place up to that point, and at the same time collect all the relevant documents. A chronology of the previous events is also necessary if for example a company has unacceptable down times for injection moulding machines produced by a specific manufacturer "A". All the relevant facts must be recorded chronologically: Which machines were bought from "A" and when? When did the breakdowns take place and how were they remedied? Who contacted "A", and when? What was discussed and decided at that time?
- Often, a simple descriptive model of the relevant part of reality is produced. For example, a toothpaste manufacturer may be surprised by turnover greatly exceeding its expectations, and therefore

Date	Events	People involved	Available documents

Figure 6.5: Grid for recording the chronology of events

have an opportunity problem. In this case, the descriptive model could consist of a customer segment - sub-market - matrix as in **Figure 6.6**. This combines customer groups/customer segments with product groups/sub-markets. As can be seen in the illustration, the boxes give figures for market volume and turnover for each of the previous two years. The market volumes are here only given as ordinal numbers and the turnovers are only of approximate values, because accounting records the turnovers of the product groups according to sales channels rather than customer segments. Despite this lack of precision, the table provides an initial overview of the decision situation.

Customer groups/ customer segments — Product groups/ sub-markets	Price-conscious toothpaste purchasers	Health-conscious purchasers	Young fashion-conscious purchasers	Parents of small children, not particularly health-conscious
Normal and fluoride toothpaste: Containing minerals and fluorides anti-cavity	* * * 0 / 0	* * 0 / 0	* * * 0 / 0	* 0 / 0
Toothpastes for gums: Containing vitamins to prevent tooth loss	* 100 / 100	* * * 200	* 380 / 400	— 0 / 0
Flavored toothpastes: Containing aromas in addition to minerals and fluorides	* 200 / 200	— 0 / 0	* * 3,200 / 4,100	* * * 1,200 / 1,600

* * * = very significant market volume
* * = significant market volume
* = reasonable market volume
— = insignificant market volume

First figure gives approximate turnover 200x-2 in thousands of euros
Second figure gives approximate turnover 200x-1 in thousands of euros

Figure 6.6: Customer segment - sub-market - matrix for the toothpaste market
(adapted from Kühn 2003)

- To systematize the data collection, it is often worth using a more complex descriptive model from the research literature. Descriptive models of this kind have also been called frames (Porter, 1991, p. 97 ff.). Frames not only indicate the variables but also often include proposals for possible cause-effect relationships. Two such frames are the five forces model (Porter, 1980, p. 3 ff.), and the value chain (Porter, 1985, p. 33 ff.).

For most decision problems, the character of the problem and its intensity changes over time. Threat problems can be expected to increase in intensity as time passes, one result of which is that a solution becomes more and more difficult and expensive until it finally becomes impossible to solve the problem at all (see **Figure 6.7**). Opportunity problems may turn into threat problems if no action is taken to exploit the opportunity, or if action is delayed too long. For example, an innovative product will find its sales possibilities greatly reduced or even annihilated once rivals with greater market power have launched similar offers. Therefore the actor should not only record the current situation but must also have an understanding of the future development of the decision situation. The actor has to forecast developments for those features of the situation subject to significant change over the period being examined. For example, if the decision-making process has been set in motion by sinking margins, then changes in market volume, in the market strength of suppliers and customers, and resulting future changes in margins must all be forecast. Normally, broad statements will be made, primarily based on subjective

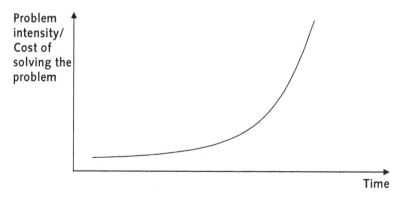

Figure 6.7: The development of a threat problem

assumptions. The development forecasts made at this stage always refer to the status quo and are thus based on the assumption that the actor will not change any decision variables.

6.2.3 Determining the causes of the problem

Causes are of interest as starting points for the development of options. From this point of view, there are two types of problem cause:

- Controllable situation variables, which can be changed by the actor and which therefore offer options for action
- Uncontrollable situation variables, which the actor must accept as given in threat problems, or may exploit to his advantage in opportunity problems

Controllable situation variables which are identified as problem causes will point directly to the areas in which to look for options to solve the problem. Examples are (1) a reward system with inadequate or unhelpful incentives or (2) ineffective advertising measures. Put differently, controllable situation features which are problem causes directly define the solution space.

Where uncontrollable situation features are identified as problem causes, such as shrinking market volume (threat problem), or a growing demand for eco-friendly products (opportunity problem), the determination of the solution space is less straightforward. With threat problems, the question is how to avoid the possible negative effects of the problem causes. With opportunity problems, there is a need to establish what measures to take in order to make the most of the opportunity. In both cases, the solution spaces can only be determined indirectly; to move towards solutions, more thought and some creativity is often required.

Finally it is possible that influenceable situation variables are identified as problem causes, for example "costs too high", "market share too low" or simply "bad business climate". These situational features do not, however, explain the problem; they only suggest, on a superficial level, possible solution spaces. They are therefore not acceptable as the outcome of analysis. As the term "influenceable" suggests, there must be specific controllable and/or uncontrollable situation features which in fact cause the "too high costs", the "bad business climate" or the "too low market share". The actor should therefore try to replace the influenceable situation variables and to identify the specific controllable and uncontrollable situation variables which effectively explain the discrepancy between current and target situations.

Further, it is worth pointing out that in the course of the process of analysis, additional decision problems may come to light, perhaps unconnected with the original problem. If solving the additional problem is found to be economically worthwhile, it may be brought into the problem-solving process. Let us consider an example of the discovery of an additional problem: the original decision process is set in motion by declining market share and its outcome will be a realignment of the marketing mix. While examining the situation feature "customers", it turns out that deliveries and customer payments do not coincide at all. Here the actor must decide whether to understand this as a problem of liquidity management and to widen the analysis accordingly.

The identification of relevant problem causes is often seen as a relatively unstructured process: hypotheses are generated, discussed in the light of the facts produced in Sub-step 2.1, and validated or discarded on this basis. However, a more structured approach to the identification of problem causes can be taken. This requires a backward-moving analysis, beginning with the discovered problem, moving back to the different levels of causes and identifying the specific causes on each of these levels.

One method for carrying out this backward-moving analysis is known as the deductive tree (Hungenberg, 1999, p. 25 ff.). Using simple logic, it divides the problem phenomenon into component areas on different levels. For each level the actor can now determine which area or areas are causing the problem and which can be excluded as irrelevant.

The Du Pont scheme in **Figure 6.8** is an example of a deductive tree. It divides the return on investment (ROI) into components. The

causes of the problem discovered by a company - a significantly reduced ROI compared with the previous year - can be determined
relatively quickly with the help of the Du Pont scheme. For example
the worsened return on investment can be attributed to lower capital
turnover, which is in turn the result of higher investment.

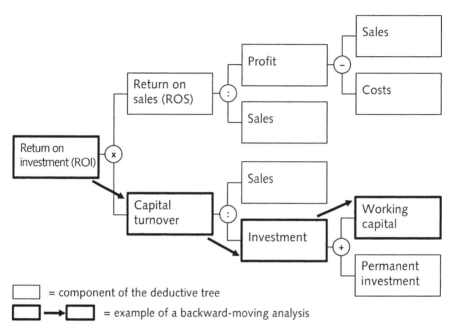

= component of the deductive tree

= example of a backward-moving analysis

Figure 6.8: The Du Pont scheme as an example of a deductive tree

Although it is not always this easy to construct a deductive tree, it is
almost always possible and useful. Another example is a problem with
greatly increased staff turnover in the research department of a phar-
maceutical manufacturer. **Figure 6.9** shows that with the help of a
deductive tree the problem can be traced back to its causes, at least
to some extent. Although the knowledge that the increased staff
turnover can essentially be attributed to the departure of university
graduates does not represent a final problem diagnosis, the actor now
knows that he needs to investigate why so many researchers with an
academic background are leaving the company.

When constructing deductive trees, the following conditions must be
respected (Hungenberg, 1999, p. 22 ff.):

- Statements at the same level cannot overlap but must exclude each other logically (exclusiveness).
- Statements at one level must be accounted for completely by the corresponding statements at the next-lowest level (exhaustiveness).

Despite the value of these restrictions, in practice deductive trees will sometimes have overlaps and/or gaps. This applies, above all, to trees with qualitative content. This is so because gaps in the actor's information base and in his/her knowledge about possible causes can, for economic reasons, never be completely filled in.

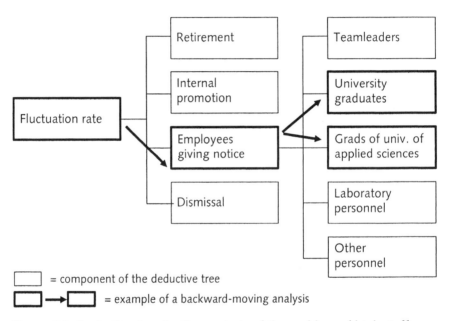

= component of the deductive tree

= example of a backward-moving analysis

Figure 6.9: Deductive tree for the analysis of the problem of high staff turnover in a research department

6.2.4   Naming the decision problem or the sub-problems

For a complex problem, Sub-step 2.2 normally leads to the identification of a number of different problem causes. These causes usually lead to the identification of a number of separate sub-problems which must be tackled, either successively or in parallel. These sub-problems must be named in Sub-step 2.3.

Problem-naming helps the actor to target the work on developing solution options. In the simplest case, problem-naming defines in a few direct words the solution space for the options. This will be possible where the central problem cause is a variable controlled by the actor. For example, if unsatisfactory performance on delivery times is identified as the cause of falling customer satisfaction, the problem can first simply be summarised as "improvement of delivery times". This problem name designates the area for improvements, a solution space which contains a number of different possible approaches to a solution: improvements in delivery planning, new policies on delivery guarantees and measures to reduce production and delivery process times. It is now sometimes a good idea to review the problem of "improvement of delivery times" once again in order to define the problem cause more closely and produce a more precise name for the problem, for example "improvement of delivery time planning". This provides a better focus for the search for solutions. The example shows that problem-naming is also useful to check the relevance of the causes identified in the previous step and to indicate whether it is necessary to loop back to improve the identification of causes.

The task of problem-naming is more complex if uncontrollable situation features, such as the pricing policies of competitors, or a decline in demand due to general economic conditions, are revealed as the principal causes of the problem. In these cases, the problem causes obviously do not offer a direct starting point for defining the solution space and for naming the problem. This means that the actor must first identify possible starting points for solving the problem. Only those situation features controlled by the actor can be considered as starting points for the search for solutions, since by definition, these are the only situation features an actor can change. Where problem causes are not controllable situation features, problem naming requires the actor to determine the most important controllable situation variables or decision variables.

If, for example, the aggressive pricing policy of the main rival is recognised as the central cause of a loss in market share, then changes in the company's own pricing policy, improvements in sales activities, changes in product quality and an intensification of advertising are possible starting points for the solution of the problem. Problem naming should include these aspects, but also leave room for related, but as yet unidentified approaches. If in doubt, it is advisable to choose a broad overall problem name, but then to append those starting points for a solution which are already clear. In the above case, the problem name could run as follows: "Reducing the negative effects of the aggressive pricing policy of our main rival by modifying or reshaping the marketing mix. Measures for improving sales activities, product quality and advertising should be examined."

Influenceable situation variables are also used for the labelling of problems or sub-problems. One speaks, for instance, of a "motivation problem", an "image problem" or of an "unsatisfactory customer retention problem". Problem names like these are the result of incomplete analysis. In principle, influenceable situation features can be traced back to variables which are either controllable or uncontrollable. Problem names with influenceable situation variables are less useful for indicating solution areas and should be avoided. In some cases, however, there is no reasonable alternative to using these features to name the problem. If a problem has a large number of possible causes, it may simply be too time-consuming or expensive to attempt a thorough analysis. In these cases the solution space remains unclear. This means that in the subsequent steps of the decision process it will be necessary to develop and assess a larger number of options.

Figure 6.10 summarises the discussion of problem naming.

6.2.5   Determining the problem structure

If a number of different sub-problems are distinguished and named, there may be dependencies between these sub-problems. Any such dependencies may need to be taken into account in the rest of the procedure.

If we assume there are two sub-problems, then there are three possible situations:
- The sub-problems can each be solved independently of the other because there are no dependencies. The marketing mix problem in

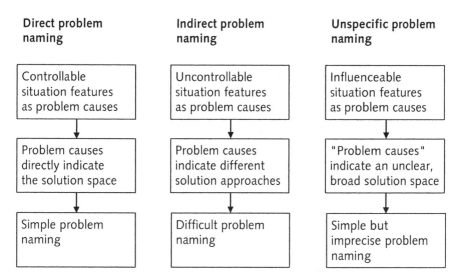

Direct problem naming	Indirect problem naming	Unspecific problem naming
Controllable situation features as problem causes	Uncontrollable situation features as problem causes	Influenceable situation features as problem causes
Problem causes directly indicate the solution space	Problem causes indicate different solution approaches	"Problem causes" indicate an unclear, broad solution space
Simple problem naming	Difficult problem naming	Simple but imprecise problem naming

Figure 6.10: Basic forms of problem naming

section 6.2.3 fits into this category, where the analysis also uncovered inadequate "liquidity management". As there are no dependencies between the content of the two problems, in principle the actor can tackle the two sub-problems at the same time in parallel. In practice however, staff time and financial resources allocated to problem solving will usually be limited, so that the actor must decide on degrees of urgency for tackling the different problems. In setting priorities the actor must take into account the financial implications of the problems, and their associated risks as well as differences in how each situation is expected to develop, that is whether the problem will intensify.

- A one-sided dependency exists whenever the solution of one sub-problem demands that the other is solved first. This situation arises when two sub-problems affect the same influenceable situation features. For example, poor motivation in a sales organisation, an influencable feature, may result from unclear targets on the one hand and inadequate performance-related salary incentives on the other. Since an incentive system is used to guarantee better attainment of goals, a clear sub-problem solution sequence results from this content-dependence: the "goal problem" must be solved before the "incentive system problem". Generally this second type of relationship between sub-problems presents no difficulties in ordering the problems. Once a dependency has been determined, a hierarchical structure necessarily follows, in which one sub-problem is subordinate to the other. Considerations of urgency are not applicable, since the subordinate problem cannot be dealt with meaningfully until a solution is found for the "higher" problem.

• Greater difficulties emerge in structuring the problem if there are interdependencies between the sub-problems rather than one-way dependencies. This occurs quite frequently in practice, because influenceable situation features - examples are customer and employee satisfaction - are often influenced by complex packages of measures. A decision problem involving poor customer or employee satisfaction may have a number of interconnected causes. In this case, the actor has two possible courses of action: the first is to tackle the two sub-problems in parallel and then later to adjust the two solutions. The alternative approach is to disregard temporarily the interdependencies and proceed by setting up a problem hierarchy. Both approaches lead to labour-intensive loops, in which earlier efforts must be repeatedly reworked.

Figure 6.11 presents the three situations of problem structuring.

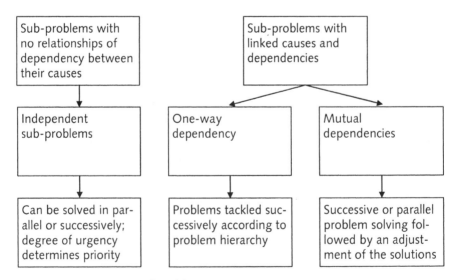

Figure 6.11: Situation of problem structuring

7 Developing and evaluating options

7.1 Developing options

7.1.1 General considerations for developing options

As **Figure 7.1** indicates, Step 3 in our general heuristic decision-making procedure is the development of options. The problem-naming represents the final sub-step in the initial analysis and provides a basis for the subsequent options. How specific the problem naming is and consequently how far the solution search is guided depends on how difficult the problem is and on the capacity of the actor to solve it. There are three possibilities:

- problem-naming can be so specific that the options are largely pre-determined,
- problem-naming can reveal the decision variables on which the options are based,
- problem-naming yields no more than very vague clues regarding possible options.

As Figure 7.1 shows, at least two options must be developed, otherwise the subsequent evaluation is meaningless. However, the requirement for at least two options seems more difficult than it is: If the continuation of the status quo is a genuine possibility, this constitutes one option. In this case the procedure requires the development of at least one further option. An example: the headquarters of an international trust is much too small and because of this it is renting office space in the surrounding area. This solution to the problem can be continued in the future. Only one additional option, for example the purchase of a larger office building, is necessary in order to produce an evaluation and selection problem.

The inclusion of the status quo offers methodological advantages. Commonly it is easier to determine what the consequences will be of maintaining the status quo than to predict the consequences of other options which are by definition new ones. It therefore makes sense to use the status quo as a baseline for evaluation and to estimate

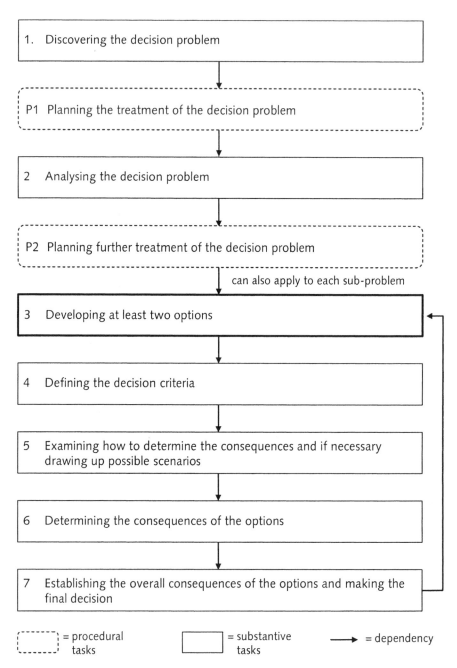

Figure 7.1: Developing at least two options in the general heuristic decision-making procedure

consequence differences for the remaining options. In design problems the development of new options typically involves great expense
- take for example the development of a new advertising concept. In
such problems it is usual to include the status quo as an option for
comparison within the first "generate and test loop".

Before work on the development of options begins, it is often useful
to specify boundary conditions: there may include restrictions on the
use of resources and measures. Decisions already taken may exclude
certain options when dealing with the new problem. For example, the
corporate strategy of a company may exclude aggressive price behaviour as an option for the businesses.

Boundary conditions restrict the solution space. It can be methodol-
ogically advantageous to have boundary conditions, especially when
at first there appears to be a variety of attractive options. In this case,
the evaluation costs can be reduced by boundary conditions, and in
extreme cases, boundary conditions are necessary in order to make a
meaningful assessment possible. However, there is also a danger: as
Figure 7.2 indicates, too many or too restrictive boundary conditions
will impede the search for solutions or produce an empty solution
space. Restraint is therefore called for when formulating conditions.
They should specify the few central limitations that are absolutely
required to make sure that options generated are both feasible and
also acceptable from a corporate viewpoint.

Provided this is not precluded by costs, a number of options should be
developed in the interests of improved solution quality. For example,
in the case of the organisation whose headquarters is too small, a
number of options can be found at an affordable cost. The possible
buildings will vary in

- location,
- size,
- ownership.

In order to be able to choose a good solution, it is important to develop clearly distinguishable options. As shown earlier in Figure 5.8, to
produce a good solution, it is necessary to develop options which

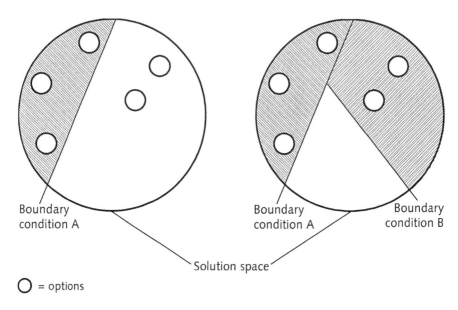

Boundary
condition A

Boundary
condition A

Boundary
condition B

Solution space

O = options

Figure 7.2: Effects of boundary conditions on the solution space

provide wide coverage of the solution space. To return to our example of a new headquarters, the option of an office building with, say,
differently designed entrance areas would not be sufficient to provide
the necessary option variety. This variety is only present if options
with different locations, sizes and ownerships are developed. The different possibilities for the entrance areas are sub-options, which
would only become of interest once that particular building had been
chosen as the solution to the initial problem.

To ensure good coverage of the solution space with a variety of options, it is advisable first to identify the most important variables of
the decision and then specify the possibilities for each of them. To do
this before attempting to define options will considerably reduce the
risk that any important solution type is neglected. This procedure is a
simplified form of Zwicky's (1966) morphological analysis, which is
explained below.

However, good coverage of the solution space does not require a
huge number of options. For each problem named in Step 2, practical
considerations suggest that no more than 6 to 8 options should be

developed and assessed. With a greater number, there is the danger that the options may differ too little from each other and that this will make evaluation difficult. Where more options are possible, it is helpful to apply the heuristic of problem factorisation. This means proceeding in two stages. In the first stage, clearly distinguishable "main options", often representing extreme positions, are identified and compared to each other. In the second stage, sub-options are developed to help to specify the preferred "main option". These sub-options sometimes integrate advantageous aspects of a main option discarded in the first step. We can illustrate this with an example. The problem is to determine the reward system for sales executives. The first stage compares three main options: "fixed compensation unrelated to performance", "results-related performance pay" and "behaviour-related performance pay". Although the main option "fixed compensation" is clearly preferred to the two performance-related pay options, it also has disadvantages. In the second stage, sub-options can be discussed which combine a substantial fixed component with limited performance-related components.

If the solution search proves difficult and the actor has the impression of having no genuine options to choose from, the use of specific techniques for the development of options should be considered. This is especially recommended when the options contain a multiplicity of decision variables or when completely new problem-solutions have to be invented. Three such techniques are introduced below.

7.1.2   Techniques for the development of options

Procedures proposed in the literature for the development of new types of options are basically creativity techniques. Three of these are introduced below:
- the ideal solution method,
- morphological boxes,
- brainstorming.

The first two of these techniques are analytical approaches which can be used by an individual or a small group. Brainstorming, in contrast, is a procedure that uses group dynamics and is best carried out in groups of six to nine people.

The first technique for promoting the discovery of new options is the development of an ideal solution. An ideal solution is a problem solution that fully satisfies all the requirements and objectives of the actor, and which, of course, can almost never be achieved in practice. However, although it is an unrealisable fiction, once the ideal solution is clearly defined and understood, the development of realisable options will be stimulated and this process can lead to options with combinations of advantages and disadvantages that were not previously available (Eisenführ & Weber, 1999, p. 79 ff.).

A second analytical method for the creative development of new options is Zwicky's (1966) morphological analysis. A matrix is used, with the decision variables on the vertical axis and their possible realisations on the horizontal. As we have seen, it always makes sense to secure good coverage of the solution space for a problem, even in cases where a completely new problem solution is not the aim. But this does not mean that the actor has to carry out a morphological analysis for every decision problem. In most cases it is enough to identify the relevant decision variables and to take account of them when formulating alternatives.

Generating options with the help of morphological analysis is a four-stage-procedure (Brauchlin, 1990, p. 302):

1. First the object of the morphological analysis is defined. When in doubt, a broader object is preferable, since a too narrow definition could exclude attractive options.
2. All important dimensions of a problem solution are listed.
3. For each of these dimensions, all possible realisations are identified.
4. Options are formulated. An option consists of a realization for each dimension.

Figure 7.3 shows a morphological matrix as a result of Steps 1 to 3 with three parameters and three, five and two realisations respectively. Based on this matrix, theoretically thirty options exist. Two of them are shown in the figure. However, normally not all of these thirty options are realisable. The figure shows an example of a combination which is not feasible.

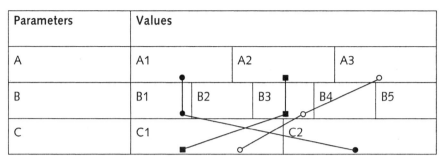

Parameters	Values					
A	A1		A2		A3	
B	B1	B2	B3		B4	B5
C	C1			C2		

● = Option I
■ = Option II
o = Impossible combination of realisations

Figure 7.3: Morphological analysis and the development of options

Brainstorming is a common method for uncovering new solutions. The search for inspiration takes place in a group session lasting 15 to 30 minutes (Brauchlin, 1990, p. 307). The participants are selected so that as many different possible areas of knowledge and experience are represented. Where possible, participants are informed beforehand about the nature of the problem that they will try to solve. The imagination should be given free rein during the brainstorming. All criticism of ideas expressed is outlawed. If one of the killer phrases listed in **Figure 7.4** is heard, the moderator has to intervene vigorously (Brauchlin 1990, p. 307 ff.).

▪ That will never work!	▪ That's already done everywhere.
▪ That's not part of company policy.	▪ That's not our problem.
▪ As if that would be accepted by the boss.	▪ That's much too complicated.
▪ That's much too expensive for us.	▪ That's much too expensive.
▪ We've already tried that.	▪ We've been doing that for ages.

Figure 7.4: Typical killer phrases
(adapted from Brauchlin, 1990, p. 306 f.)

7.2   Defining the decision criteria

As **Figure 7.5** shows, establishing the decision criteria or types of consequences is the fourth sub-problem in the general heuristic decision-

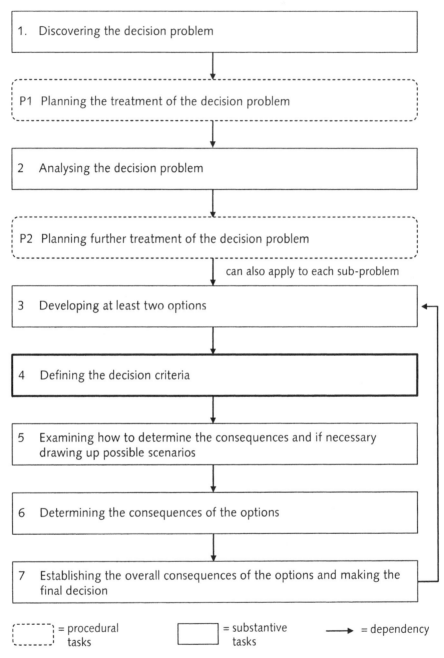

Figure 7.5: Defining the decision criteria in the general heuristic decision-making procedure

making procedure. A decision criterion is the specification of a goal relevant to the evaluation of the options in a decision problem. Together the various decision criteria form a framework for the evaluation of the options. The criteria should be influenceable situation variables which are relevant to the superordinate goals to which the decision is subject.

Since a goal system usually includes a number of different objectives, a number of different decision criteria are required when evaluating options. Each objective can be represented by one or more decision criteria. For example, when evaluating rationalisation projects the goal of "increasing productivity" can be measured as "units per man-hour". But, in the context of rationalisation, when evaluating the goal "quality of the working process", the two different criteria "waste" and "downtime" could be employed in parallel.

If, exceptionally, the evaluation of options is based on a single decision criterion, then this is referred to as a univalent decision problem. When there is more than one decision criterion, but the criteria stand in a mathematical relationship to each other, then this is also a univalent decision problem. Imagine, for example, a decision about product range options which is based on the two decision criteria "net income per item" and "variable costs per item". The evaluation of the options might just as well be based on the difference between the values for the two criteria, that is, the contribution margin per item.

If there is more than one decision criterion and they do not bear a mathematical relationship to each other, then this is referred to as a polyvalent decision. When evaluating options, polyvalent decisions are the norm.

Decision criteria should satisfy two conditions:
- A good decision criterion must adequately represent a goal, or at least a part of a goal. This condition is met if the decision criterion "item per man-hour" is used to evaluate the productivity of rationalisation investments. The two decision criteria "waste" and "downtime" also meet this requirement if used to evaluate the quality of rationalisation projects. On its own, neither criterion is able to represent the goal satisfactorily, but together, they should

represent the quality of the working process as a result of rationalisation investment quite well.

- A good decision criterion must clearly show how the options are evaluated. In contrast to a goal, where a less precise idea of the content is acceptable, for a decision criterion, the actor requires a precise idea of what is meant. When there is a clear idea of how the decision options are to be judged in relation to the criterion, it can be referred to as an operational criterion. Let us suppose that user-friendliness of mobile phones is being measured on the basis of a comparison to a widely distributed Nokia model. The actor may then define three values: "more user-friendly", "equally user-friendly" and "less user-friendly". The three criteria mentioned above, "unit per man-hour", "waste" and "downtime", also qualify as operational decision criteria (Heinen, 1976, p. 115 ff.).

The requirement for operationality of the decision criteria has an important consequence on the order of the steps in our general heuristic decision-making procedure: the requirement means that the options must first be developed before the decision criteria can be fixed. This is because it is only after the options are known that a sufficiently reliable assessment can be made as to whether any particular decision criterion will allow the evaluation of the options with the required precision. The authors consider this a central point. However, it is clear that, from a purely logical point of view, the order of the sub-problems in our procedure can be criticised, because the evaluation criteria are not defined until the options as objects of the evaluation are known. With this sequence, there is the risk that the evaluation criteria will be defined in such a way that the intuitively preferred option will come out on top in the subsequent evaluation. But our view is that this risk is not overcome simply by placing the fixing of the decision criteria before the development of options. This is because the heuristic procedure makes it possible to loop back at the end of each step to sub-tasks completed earlier and so in no way prevents revision and expansion of the list of criteria after the development of the options. Thus the danger of manipulation exists independently of the order of the sub-tasks in the problem-solving procedure.

If the evaluation of consequences is based on more than one decision criterion, the actor must ensure that he/she uses criteria which are independent of each other and do not overlap. Otherwise the actor may use two criteria to measure the same effects of the options twice, so that effects in a particular area are counted double. An example would be a decision about changing the organisational structure, for which "effects on employee satisfaction" and "effects on employee motivation" are used as two separate decision criteria. These two criteria are not independent measures, as there are cause-effect relationships between them. The actor should therefore decide in favour of the more important criterion. If this is hard to do, a way to overcome the difficulty is to weight these two criteria lower than the other independent criteria. We return to the topic of the weighting of criteria in the next chapter when we look at decision maxims for polyvalent decisions.

7.3   Examining how to determine the consequences and if necessary drawing up possible scenarios

When speaking of the consequences of options, we mean their effects on those specific influenceable situation variables selected as decision criteria. The effects of an option begin once the decision has been made and these effects normally last much longer than the period of implementation. In many decision problems, only an approximate estimate can be made as to the relevant time period for assessing the consequences of options. **Figure 7.6** summarises this situation.

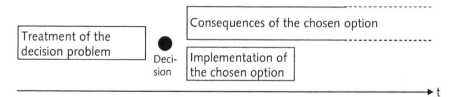

Figure 7.6: Temporal sequence showing the decision-making process, the decision, the implementation and the consequences

Before attempting to predict the consequences of the options, it is helpful to examine a number of general issues and perhaps to draw up scenarios on which to base the examination of the consequences.

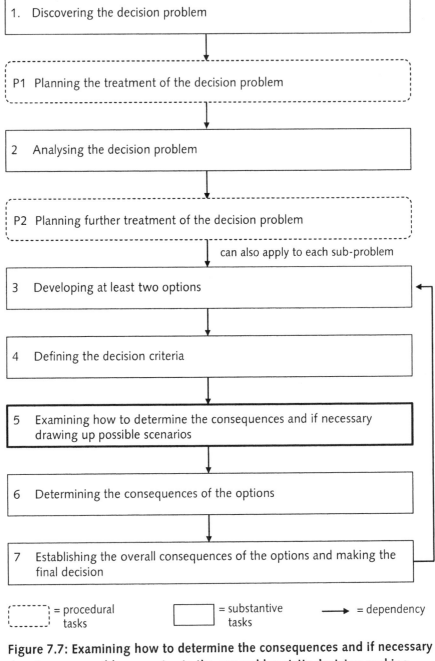

Figure 7.7: Examining how to determine the consequences and if necessary drawing up possible scenarios in the general heuristic decision-making procedure

These tasks are represented as step 5 in the general heuristic decision-making procedure, as shown in **Figure 7.7**.

It seems sensible to divide Step 5 into three sub-steps, as indicated in **Figure 7.8**.

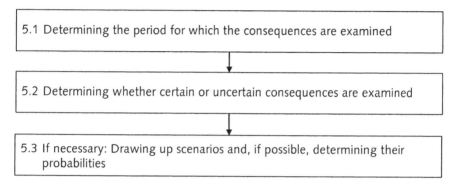

5.1 Determining the period for which the consequences are examined

5.2 Determining whether certain or uncertain consequences are examined

5.3 If necessary: Drawing up scenarios and, if possible, determining their probabilities

Figure 7.8: Sub-steps in Step 5

Sub-step 5.1 requires the actor to determine the period for which the effects of the options are to be predicted. Since the effects of the options normally decrease with time, the period for the examination of the consequences can be cut off after a certain time without this producing any significant errors of judgement. However, it is often difficult to resolve exactly where this point lies and thus how long the period should be for which the effects of the options are determined. Often the answer to this question will be based on a subjective judgment. But there are also decision problems for which a clear basis exists for fixing this time horizon. In investment decisions, for example, the planned use of a potential investment product will determine for how long the consequences should be recorded.

In Sub-step 5.2 the actor has to decide whether to establish a single value for the consequences of each option and for each decision criterion or whether to have a range of values.

- If the actor assumes that the effects of an option are more or less certain, then only one consequence value per option and per decision criterion will be required.

- If, for one or more decision criteria, uncontrollable situation variables suggest that the effects are uncertain, then more than one
  value will be required for each option and criterion.

In the first case, we can speak of a decision which is certain. In the
second case, we distinguish two types of decision according to
whether the actor is able to determine probabilities for the different
values. If probabilities can be determined then there is a decision under risk; if no probabilities can be established, then the decision is
uncertain.

If in sub-step 5.2, the actor comes to the conclusion that at least
some consequence values are risky or uncertain, then it is necessary to
create a clear basis on which to determine these risky or uncertain
consequence values. This is Sub-task 5.3, in which a number of different scenarios are defined, for which consequence values can then be
determined.

Two routes are open to the actor to achieve this. If there are numerous uncertain and uncontrollable situation variables whose effects for
the consequences of options are difficult to predict, then the actor can
define scenarios directly. To investigate the consequences of market-
entry options in France, for example, one could create three scenarios:
one optimistic, one moderate, and one pessimistic. These scenarios
group together factors such as general economic conditions, tax legis-
lation, demand for the product, the exchange rate of the euro, and
many other environmental features. Where there is only a small number of uncontrollable situation variables which have a significant influence on the consequences, then the following step-by-step procedure
is recommended:

- First, identify the variables that have a significant influence on the
  consequences of the options and which are uncertain. It is possible
  that there is only one uncertain situation variable. For instance, for
  the launch of a new product, the factor might be the general economic situation or for a decision about a product development, it
  might be the ability to patent the product. But there may be a
  number of uncertain situation variables which have a significant influence. For example the economic viability of a project for the installation of new chair and ski lifts will depend to a great extent on
  the amount of snow in winter, on the temperature and rainfall in
  summer and on the development of tourist demand in the region.

- Next, summarize the uncertain situation variables into scenarios. The decision about whether to launch a new product can be based on three economic scenarios, according to different growth rates for the GDP. A poor economic situation could be set as negative growth, a moderate situation could see growth from 0% to 2% and anything greater than 2% would be a good economic situation. Drawing up scenarios is somewhat more difficult if there are a number of uncertain situation variables with significance for evaluating the options. In this case, the scenarios should present combinations of values or ranges of values for the different uncertain situation variables. **Inset 7.1** presents the formation of scenarios as a basis for the judgement of projects for the installation of new chair and ski lifts.
- Finally check whether probabilities can be assigned to the scenarios. The assignment of probabilities is not absolutely necessary and should therefore only be carried out if the probabilities can be supported by facts. For the weather scenarios in the context of the chair and ski lift projects for example, one would be able to assign probabilities using meteorological records. But it probably does not make sense to assign probabilities to the two scenarios of patenting succeeding or not succeeding. If it is clear to everyone whether the new discovery is worthy of a patent, then one need not bother with the scenarios. If the question of patenting is doubtful however, and the two scenarios are therefore required, it will be difficult to make a reliable statement of their respective probabilities.

Inset 7.1: Determining environmental scenarios as a basis for evaluating chair and ski lift projects

A number of renovation projects have been proposed for a small ski station with outdated chair and ski lifts. They differ in two respects. The first is whether all existing installations should be torn down or some preserved. The second is the question of capacity. The economic evaluation of these proposals will be based on varying scenarios for future climatic conditions.

The actor assumes that three uncertain situation variables will have a significant influence on the economic success of the chair and ski lift projects:

- weather in the winter,
- weather in the summer,
- snow conditions in the winter.

On the other hand, the actor assumes that the expected tourist demand for the region will not change, so that this variable does not need to be taken into account.

To draw up the scenarios we proceed as follows:

- Because the installation is out of service in November for general maintenance work, there are 335 business days per year. As it is important to take account of the demand for skiing, these days are divided into 100 in the winter season and 235 in the summer season.
- On the basis of meteorological data, it is possible to distinguish between poor, average and good seasons for both winter and summer. Each category will consist of a mix of poor, average and good days. The difference between a poor, an average and a good summer or winter will be found in the relative proportions of each category, so that a good summer has 96 good days, for example, and only 56 poor days, while a bad summer has only 68 good days as against 70 poor days.
- For the winter season, the poor, average and good weather days are additionally classified as days with poor, average or good snow conditions.
- **Figure 7.9** shows the result of this analysis. The table shows the average number of days classified as poor, average or good for both weather and snow conditions.
- A total of nine scenarios can be drawn up on this basis: poor winter/poor summer, poor winter/average summer, poor winter/good summer, and so on.

Meteorological records suggest that an average winter or summer is twice as likely to occur as a poor or good winter or summer. This gives the following probabilities for the nine scenarios:

- poor winter and summer 0.0625
- poor winter and average summer: 0.125
- poor winter and good summer: 0.0625
- average winter and poor summer: 0.125
- average winter and summer: 0.25

Quality of winter and summer	Number of days		Classification of days according to weather and snow quality											
	Winter	Summer	Winter									Summer		
			Snow											
			Poor			Average			Good			Poor	Average	Good
			Poor	Average	Good	Poor	Average	Good	Poor	Average	Good			
Poor winter	100		6	12	6	11	23	12	7	15	8			
Average winter	100		5	11	6	11	22	12	8	16	9			
Good winter	100		5	10	5	11	22	11	9	18	9			
Poor summer		235										70	97	68
Average summer		235										63	90	82
Good summer		235										56	83	96

Figure 7.9: Good, average and poor winter and summer

- average winter and good summer: 0.125
- good winter and poor summer: 0.0625
- good winter and average summer: 0.125
- good winter and good summer: 0.0625

On the basis of the frequency of the different types of days visitor numbers and turnovers can be estimated for the different scenarios. These nine scenarios thus define the required consequences and also allow us to calculate the corresponding values.

7.4   The configuration of the decision problem as result of steps 3, 4 and 5

In steps 3, 4 and 5 all the elements are identified which are necessary to allow us to configure the decision problem in the form of a decision matrix:

- In step 3 the options are formulated. These will have to be compared and evaluated.
- In step 4 the criteria are established for this evaluation.
- If needed, in step 5, scenarios are drawn up and where possible, the probabilities of the scenarios are determined.

The results of these three steps specify the problem, which can now be configured as a decision matrix. **Figure 7.10** presents a decision matrix for the evaluation of options for the expansion of a company owned by a Polish family settled in Switzerland. The company has only been active in Switzerland up to now. As can be seen from the illustration, four options have been developed and must be assessed against two decision criteria.

For one of the two criteria, the consequences depend on whether the integration of the planned subsidiary abroad succeeds and thus the hoped-for synergies can be realized. Two scenarios are therefore proposed: "Integration goes well" and "Integration goes badly".

Criteria and scenarios	C_1: Discounted cash flow of the next 5 years in millions of euro		C_2: Creation of jobs in Poland (*)
	S_1: Integration goes well	S_2: Integration goes badly	
Options			
O_1: Buy manufacturer U with production plants in Germany and Poland	c_{111}	c_{112}	c_{12}
O_2: Buy manufacturer V with a production plant in Poland and sales agencies in Germany	c_{211}	c_{212}	c_{22}
O_3: Create new sales agencies in Germany and Poland for products from Switzerland	c_{311}	c_{312}	c_{32}
O_4: No expansion	c_{41}		c_{42}

O_x = Options
C_y = Criteria
S_z = Scenarios
c_{xy} = Single consequence of option x in relation to criterion y
c_{xyz} = Single consequence of option x in relation to criterion y and scenario z
(*)   Measure on the ordinal scale with the categories "very many", "many", "some", "few" and "none"

Figure 7.10: Example of an empty decision matrix

A decision problem always requires at least two options. But these options need not be evaluated against multiple criteria, as in this case.

As we have already seen, there are univalent and polyvalent decision problems:

- A univalent decision problem is one in which the evaluation of the options is carried out on the basis of a single decision criterion or of multiple criteria which stand in a mathematical relationship to each other.
- A polyvalent decision problem is one in which there is more than one decision criterion and the criteria are not mathematically related.

The scenarios presented in Figure 7.9 are also not obligatory. As we have seen, there are three possibilities.

- There are no uncertain situation features with significant influence on the problem. In this case we have a certain decision.
- Among the variables with significance for the evaluation of options, there are one or more which are uncertain. Scenarios are drawn up on the basis of these variables. If probabilities can be established for the scenarios, the decision is under risk.
- There is more than one scenario and probabilities cannot be assigned. The resulting decision is uncertain.

Since decisions may be univalent or polyvalent on the one hand and can be classified as certain, risky and uncertain on the other hand, there are therefore six possible decision configurations, represented in **Figure 7.11**.

7.5   Determining the consequences of the options

As **Figure 7.12** shows, the sixth step in the general heuristic decision-making procedure is determining the effects or consequences of the various options. In this step the difficulty is not so much a methodological one, but lies in establishing reliable knowledge about the

	Univalent decision	Polyvalent decision
Certain decision	Certain univalent decision	Certain polyvalent decision
Risky decision	Risky univalent decision	Risky polyvalent decision
Uncertain decision	Uncertain univalent decision	Uncertain polyvalent decision

Figure 7.11: The six decision types

decision situation. This is perhaps the reason why the literature hardly touches on the task of determining the single consequences of options.

As we have seen, the decision problem is structured through steps 3, 4 and 5. On the basis of these three steps, a specific decision matrix can be produced. The decision matrix, an example of which was introduced in Figure 7.10, is central for determining consequences. All the single effects of the options which need to be determined follow directly from it, so that the results of step 6 proceed from the matrix in a clearly structured way.

Determining the consequences means making a prognosis of future states or of changes in influenceable situation variables. These prognoses are always based on understandings about cause-effect-relationships acquired in the past. The assumption that such understandings will continue to be valid allows statements to be made about the future. Thus the reliability of consequences depends on the quality of the cause-effect-models that the actor uses. In practice it is useful to distinguish three quality levels when determining consequences:

- Frequently, actors are content to make subjective assessments on the basis of experience. This approach is reasonable when there are many different individual effects to determine or if the application of predictive models would be too expensive or time-consuming.

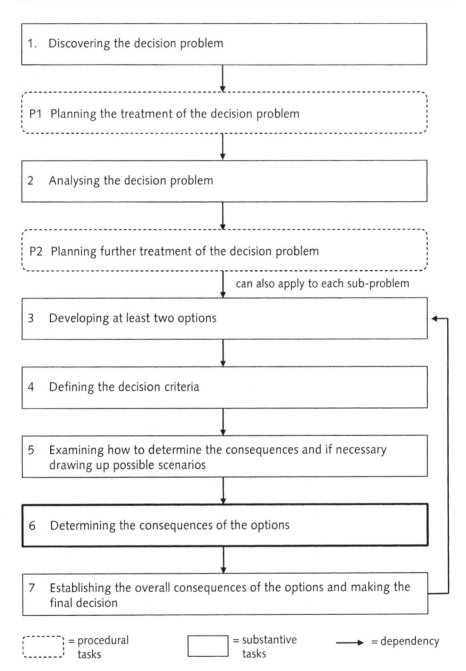

Figure 7.12: Determining the consequences of the options in the general heuristic decision-making procedure

But even where subjective appraisal is used, the actor should always take into account those cause-effect relationships uncovered through problem analysis in step 2.

- A higher level of quality is achieved when carrying out empirical studies on option effects. For example, specifically targeted market research can determine the possible effects of TV ads or of different packaging. It is also possible to carry out a survey, for instance, to see how employees will react to alternative designs of their reward system. Other examples of determining consequences at this second level are empirically supported calculations of costs and practical testing of prototypes. The data collection or testing should be recent. The use of survey or test findings in determining consequences is based on the assumption that these effects will not change significantly for the chosen time period of the consequences.

- The highest level of quality is achieved when the effects of options are determined with scientifically verified predictive methods. For this to be possible, there must be reliable empirically and/or theoretically grounded explanatory models which explain the relationships between the most important variables of the situation. Models of this kind are available primarily for purely technical problems in which the laws of natural science play a central role. With complex business management decision problems the most one can hope for is to have scientific predictive models to identify some part of the relevant consequences. For example, a statistically based demand function could be used to evaluate the demand consequences of a range of alternative prices. Or an advertising effect model could be used to determine the optimal advertising budget. In some cases at least the consequences of the status quo alternative can be determined on the basis of an extrapolation. However, in complex business management problems, it is rare that such firmly-grounded predictive models are available.

In most cases, there is no alternative to an intuitive estimate of the consequences because empirical methods and prescriptive models are either impossible or too expensive. This is problematic because people normally overrate their knowledge and therefore tend to trust their subjective judgements too much: "It's not what we don't know that gives us trouble, it's what we know that ain't so." (Will Rogers, cited in Russo/Schoemaker, 1990, p. 95).

This tendency to overestimate one's own knowledge has to be countered. For reliable evaluations of options the following measures appear to be useful:

- As explained in Chapter 5, the consequences can first be determined independently by a number of individuals. Each person is then confronted with the judgements of the others and the differences are worked out. This is similar to a Delphi study but much less costly and leads to a group judgement that is fundamentally better than the individual judgements. The group judgement is also better than a simple averaging of individual judgements because erroneous ideas are uncovered in the discussion and individuals can revise their judgements.
- Group discussion can be stimulated by asking disconfirming questions. These questions can doubt the experience and knowledge on which the evaluation is based or can doubt the assumptions underlying the consequences (Russo/Schoemaker, 1990, p. 103 ff.).
- It is also important to confront those responsible for determining the consequences with the real effects of the chosen option. Learning effects can be achieved in this way that will have a positive effect in a subsequent, similar decision problem (Russo/Schoemaker, 1990, p. 98 ff.).

8   Establishing the overall consequences of the options and making the final decision

8.1   General considerations

The last step in the heuristic decision-making procedure represents a double task: establishing the overall consequences of the options and making the final decision. However **Figure 8.1** shows that a heuristic loop can occur if the evaluation does not produce an option that satisfies the requirements of the actor, but hope remains that better options can still be found. In this case the procedure proposes working through Steps 3 to 7 once again. If the heuristic has developed only one option and this is compared with the status quo in Step 7, it is highly likely that several run-throughs will take place. It would be a fortunate accident if the first solution corresponded to the actor's requirements.

The starting point for Step 7 completes the decision matrix. Options, decision criteria, scenarios and consequence values can all be seen in the matrix. In some circumstances, the decision matrix will also provide probabilities for the scenarios. **Figure 8.2** shows the decision matrix from section 7.4, now completed with consequence values for the three options.

On the basis of a completed decision matrix like the one in Figure 8.2, two different courses of action are possible:
- The options can summarily be judged on the basis of the individual consequences. Here the overall judgements are normally formulated in words, but should allow the options to be ranked, thus making the decision possible.
- The individual consequences of the options are first summarised analytically with the help of one or two decision maxims. The resulting overall consequences then form the basis for the decision.

In the case of a problem which is certain and univalent, there is no question of whether to proceed summarily or analytically: the consequences of the options are the same as the overall consequences and

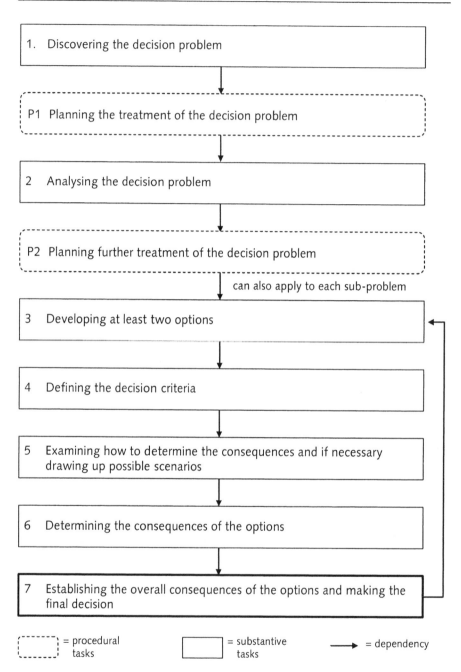

Figure 8.1: Establishing the overall consequences of the options and making the final decision in the general heuristic decision-making procedure

Criteria and scenarios	C_1: Discounted cash flow of the next 5 years in millions of euro		C_2: Creation of jobs in Poland (*)
Options	S_1: Integration goes well	S_2: Integration goes badly	
O_1: Buy manufacturer U with production plants in Germany and Poland	$c_{111} = 10$	$c_{112} = -4$	$c_{12} =$ many
O_2: Buy manufacturer V with a production plant in Poland and sales agencies in Germany	$c_{211} = 5$	$c_{212} = -2$	$c_{22} =$ very many
O_3: Create new sales agencies in Germany and Poland for products from Switzerland	$c_{311} = 2$	$c_{312} = 0$	$C_{32} =$ few
O_4: No expansion	$c_{41} = 0$		$c_{42} =$ none

O_x = Options
C_y = Criteria
S_z = Scenarios
c_{xy} = Single consequence of option x in relation to criterion y
c_{xyz} = Single consequence of option x in relation to criterion y and scenario z
(*)   Measure on the ordinal scale with the categories "very many", "many", "some", "few" and "none"

Figure 8.2: Example of a completed decision matrix

thus directly form the basis for the decision. **Figure 8.3** shows the decision matrix of a certain univalent decision problem: a trading company has to decide which of three mutually exclusive products should be included in the range. It is assumed that all three items will yield the same quantitative sales and that the actor can therefore judge on the basis of the contribution margin per unit. Since the contribution margin represents not only the individual consequence but also the overall consequence, it is not necessary to determine whether the actor should make a summary judgement or should first establish the overall consequences of the options with decision maxims.

Options of products to be included in the range	Contribution margin per unit in Swiss francs as consequences
Option A	50
Option B	61
Option C	46

Figure 8.3: Example of a completed decision matrix for a certain univalent decision

For polyvalent and risky or uncertain decisions the literature generally recommends an analytic procedure, using one or more decision maxims. To determine the overall consequences analytically, a quantitative value has to be established for each of the consequences, including those which are qualitative in nature. This raises the question of whether the actor is willing to trust the overall consequences of the options, given that these may depend on a great number of different calculations. This is especially important where the decision is a very important one. There are cases in which the actor better fulfils his responsibility by proceeding on the basis of a summary judgment of the individual consequences of the options. All this means that, for each decision, the actor has to come to a conclusion about which of the two approaches, summarizing or analytical, best suits the particular problem and the degree of responsibility involved.

Summary assessment of the individual consequences of the options can also produce sound decisions. This is because an actor who has systematically carried through Steps 1 to 6 of the procedure will normally have clear ideas of the main advantages and disadvantages of the options. Moreover the actor can improve his/her assessment by reducing the complexity of the decision matrix. Many decision matrices contain options which are inferior to other options on all criteria. These can be eliminated at once. There will also be criteria with the same or only marginally different consequences for the various options. These criteria and the consequences assigned to them can also be excluded from further consideration as they will not influence the decision. Finally the decision matrix can be simplified by summarising those individual consequences that are arithmetically related.

Even with a potentially reduced decision matrix, sometimes the actor cannot make a clear decision on the basis of a summary judgement of the options. Additionally, the quality of the summary decision may be suspect for other reasons. Should this occur, there is nothing to stop the actor from backtracking and now proceeding analytically to obtain a second decision which can be compared with the first judgement.

In comparison to other steps in decision-making, the analytical procedures used in determining the overall consequences of options have perhaps received too much attention in books on decision-making. Here we provide a relatively brief treatment. Our aim is to explain and demonstrate the decision maxims so that the reader will be able to apply them. Detailed explanation of the assumptions underlying the maxims and justification for their use is not provided here.

8.2   Overview of the decision maxims and their applicability

The following sections of this chapter present approaches to the analytical evaluation of options, beginning in section 8.2 with an overview of the decision maxims for the establishment of the overall consequences and indications of when each maxim can be applied. After this, sections 8.3 to 8.5 introduce the three different categories of decision maxims and provide examples of how they can be applied. In section 8.6 we explain how to use decision maxims in combination in order to tackle problems which are both polyvalent, and also risky or uncertain. Finally in section 8.7 the chapter concludes with an account of the advantages and disadvantages of the different maxims.

As outlined in section 7.4, six different decision configurations can be identified. **Figure 8.4** shows the decision maxims which apply to each of the six types:

- For univalent/certain decisions, no decision maxim is necessary. The consequences of the options are the same as their overall consequences.

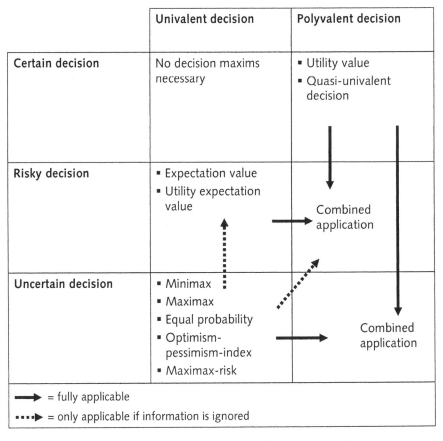

Figure 8.4 : The different decision maxims and their applications

- For univalent risky decisions the expectation value can be calculated. Bernoulli has developed a procedure which takes into account the actor's attitude to risk. It is also possible to apply the maxims for uncertain decisions. However, this is only possible if some information is ignored, since the different scenarios are considered without their probabilities of occurrence.
- For univalent uncertain decisions three approaches, the maximax, Wald's minimax and Laplace's equal probability may each be used as simple maxims for establishing the overall consequences. Hurwicz's optimism-pessimism index and Savage and Niehans' minimax risk maxim may also be used, but these are more demanding maxims.
- With polyvalent certain decisions, a maxim to overcome the polyvalence is needed. Available maxims are the utility value and the examination of the decision problem as quasi-univalent.
- In the case of polyvalent risky problems, a maxim to overcome polyvalence is combined with a maxim to overcome uncertainty. Additionally, instead of using a maxim to overcome the risk situation, it is possible to use a maxim to overcome uncertainty. Here again information must be ignored.
- Finally, polyvalent uncertain decisions need a combination of a maxim to overcome polyvalence and a maxim to overcome uncertainty.

In sections 8.3 to 8.5 the range of maxims for overcoming polyvalence and risk and uncertainty will be introduced. But first we will see how the actor can reduce the task by eliminating some options directly on the basis of the completed decision matrix. With polyvalent decisions this is always possible if one option performs worse than another on all criteria. With risky and uncertain problems, an option can be excluded if it represents worse consequences than another option for all scenarios. In these cases, one speaks of natural order: **Inset 8.1** presents two examples.

Inset 8.1: Natural orders

The application of one or more decision maxims to establish the overall consequences of the options involves a certain amount of effort. Before this work is embarked upon, the decision matrix for establishing the consequences of options should be checked for natural order. A natural order is present, if one option rates below another in every criterion or is partly below and partly equivalent, so that the actor can exclude this option without considering its overall consequences.

Figure 8.5 shows an example of natural order in the case of a polyvalent/certain decision. As can be seen from the illustration, tool machine A rates below tool machine B in every aspect. It can therefore be eliminated without investigation of its overall consequences. Consequently, the actor will only have to decide between the tool machines B and C and/or the status quo, if needed.

Decision criteria Options	Investment in Swiss francs	Capacity in items per hour	Precision in mm	Safety level
Tool machine A	550,000	1,000	± 0.2	good
Tool machine B	500,000	1,200	± 0.1	very good
Tool machine C	480,000	1,050	± 0.15	satisfactory

Figure 8.5: Example of a natural order in a polyvalent certain decision problem

But natural order also comes into play in the four other configurations: univalent/risky, univalent/uncertain, polyvalent/risky and polyvalent/uncertain.

Figure 8.6 shows an example of a natural order in the case of a polyvalent/uncertain decision. Since only two options exist and option B outperforms option A in every area, the decision can be taken without investigation of the overall consequences. The actor is thus spared the task of applying two decision maxims, one to overcome polyvalence and one to overcome uncertainty.

Criteria and scenarios / Options	Project cost in Swiss francs		Cumulative profits for next five years in Swiss francs		Technology gain
	Patenting succeeds	Patenting fails	Patenting succeeds	Patenting fails	
Development project A	480,000	440,000	1,250,000	625,000	high
Development project B	430,000	390,000	1,500,000	975,000	very high

Figure 8.6: Example of a natural order in a polyvalent uncertain decision problem

8.3   Decision maxims for overcoming polyvalence

8.3.1   Utility value maxim

Utility value maxim (Bamberg & Coenenberg, 2002, p. 47 ff.; Eisenführ & Weber, 1999, p. 113 ff.; Rommelfanger & Eickemeier, 2002, p. 140 ff.) is used in the following way:

1. The consequence values are transformed into utility values. This must be done for each consequence type. In order to avoid indirectly weighting the consequence values, each consequence type gets the same sum of utility values. It is recommended to work with "1" as the sum of the utility values of a consequence type. This means that for each consequence type, the utility value for each option lies between 0 and 1. It makes sense to award the highest utility value for the most favourable and the lowest utility value for the most unfavourable consequence. With the purchase of a vehicle, this would mean in reference to price, for example, that the vehicle with the lowest price has the highest utility value.

2. The second step consists of the weighting of the consequence types. Subjective judgements are required to produce weightings which reflect the relative importance of the criteria for the attain-

ment of the goal(s). To standardize the weighting of the consequence types, we propose fixing the sum of all weightings at "1".
3. Now that the consequence values have been transformed into utility values and the weightings for the decision criteria/consequence
types have been determined, the overall consequences can be established. To do this, the utility values are multiplied by their
weightings and the weighted utility values are added together.

The most difficult and costly step in the application of the utility value
maxim is certainly the first one. **Inset 8.2** shows how the transformation of the consequence values into utility values can be carried out
for different categories of decision criteria/consequence types.

Inset 8.2: Transforming consequence values into utility values

When calculating utility values from consequence values, four different consequence types are distinguished:
- Quantitative consequence types where a high value is positive,
  such as the contribution margin.
- Quantitative consequence types where a high value is negative,
  such as costs.
- Qualitative consequence types where a high evaluation is positive, such as aesthetics.
- Qualitative consequence types where a high evaluation is negative, such as offensive odours.

In the main text, we recommend that for all consequence types the
sum of the utility values should be 1. In this way no indirect
weighting occurs.

The calculation of utility values proceeds differently for each of the
four consequence types:
- Quantitative positive consequence types, like profit, are transformed into utility values by expressing the values for the individual consequences as a proportion of the sum of all the values.
- Quantitative negative consequence values, such as costs, are
  transformed into utility values by first determining the reciprocal
  for each consequence value. The reciprocal of a number is 1 di-

vided by that number. The reciprocals are then expressed as a proportion of the sum of all the reciprocals. Let us take an example: a student is looking for a new apartment and has three options to choose from. The monthly rent is a decision criterion/consequence type. **Figure 8.7** shows the three figures for rent and their transformation into utility values. In this procedure the apartment with the lowest rent has the highest utility value and the apartment with the highest rent has the lowest utility value.

Option	Rent in Swiss francs	Reciprocal of the rent	Utility value
Apartment A	1,000	0.001	0.32
Apartment B	1,100	0.000909	0.29
Apartment C	800	0.00125	0.39
Total	–	0.003159	1.00

Figure 8.7: Example of the transformation of quantitative negative consequences into utility values

- Qualitative positive consequence types, such as aesthetics, are first transformed into quantitative values by using a defined scale. The quantitative values must reflect the "distances" between the verbal consequence values as well as possible. Utility values can then be calculated in the same way as for quantitative positive consequence values. We return to the example above. Alongside rental costs, the student has chosen comfort as a further decision criterion and has rated the three apartments on a qualitative scale with four values "excellent", "very good", "good" and "satisfactory". **Figure 8.8** gives the evaluations and their subsequent transformation into utility values. As the illustration shows, although the evaluation of living comfort is based on a four-point scale, none of the apartments has been given the value "very good". This fact must be taken into account when converting the verbal consequences into numerical values, because the distance between "excellent" and "good" is twice as far as the distance between "good" and "satisfactory".

Option	Living comfort	Quantitative value of living comfort	Utility value
Apartment A	good	2	0.29
Apartment B	excellent	4	0.57
Apartment C	satisfactory	1	0.14
Total	–	7	1.00

Measured on the following scale: "excellent", "very good", "good" and "satisfactory"

Figure 8.8: Example of the transformation of qualitative positive consequences into utility values

- Qualitative negative consequence types, such as offensive odours, are first converted into quantitative values using a rating scale. In this conversion, the negative consequence type is transformed into a positive consequence type, as the most disadvantageous consequence is assigned the smallest quantitative value and the most advantageous the largest quantitative value. Here too one should make sure that the "distances" between values are represented satisfactorily. The transformation into utility values can afterwards be carried out in the same way as for quantitative positive consequence types.

With quantitative consequence types, both positive and negative, the consequence values may extend from negative values through zero to positive values. This is possible for example with the consequence type "Return on Investment" (ROI). This makes the conversion into utility values proposed above impossible. To counter this difficulty, the consequence values must be transformed into a value area $\geq$ 0 before they are converted into utility values. This is possible for all consequence values by adding a constant. The increase in the consequence values is unproblematic because the utility values represent values on an interval scale. **Figure 8.9** provides an example in which four potential acquisitions are assessed, among other things, on the basis of their ROI for the previous year. The results obtained extend from negative to positive values. The illustration shows how these ROI are transformed into utility values.

Option	ROI	Transformed ROI	Utility value
Acquisition A	8%	10%	0.53
Acquisition B	- 2%	0%	0.00
Acquisition C	0%	2%	0.10
Acquisition D	5%	7%	0.37
Total	-	19%	1.00

Figure 8.9: Example of the transformation of consequences with positive and negative values into utility values

The utility value maxim is now applied to the example of a student who has to choose from three apartments. **Figure 8.10** shows his decision matrix with three consequence types. The three consequence types have different qualities:

- Living space is a quantitative positive consequence.
- Rent is quantitative, negative consequence.
- Living comfort is a qualitative, positive consequence.

Figure 8.11 shows the result of applying the maxim:

- First, the consequence values are transformed into utility values. The sum of the utility values of a consequence type is 1.

Decision criteria / Option	Rent in Swiss francs	Living space in m^2	Living comfort
Apartment A	1,000	120	good
Apartment B	1,100	120	excellent
Apartment C	800	90	satisfactory

Figure 8.10: Example of the utility value maxim: starting point

- Next the consequence types are given weightings.
- Finally, the weighted utility values are calculated and added for each option. Since the sum of the utility values of each consequence type is 1 and the weightings also total 1, the sum of the weighted utility values of the three options is also 1.

On the basis of the sum of the weighted utility values, apartment B can be chosen.

Decision criteria and weightings / Options	Rent in Swiss francs	Living space in m^2	Living comfort	Total of the weighted utility values
	0.5	0.3	0.2	
Apartment A	0.32 0.16	0.36 0.11	0.29 0.06	– 0.33
Apartment B	0.29 0.14	0.36 0.11	0.57 0.11	– 0.36
Apartment C	0.39 0.20	0.28 0.08	0.14 0.03	– 0.31
Total	1.00 0.5	1.00 0.3	1.00 0.2	– 1.00
Upper figures = utility values Lower figures = weighted utility values				

Figure 8.11: Example of the utility value maxim: calculation

8.3.2   The maxim of the quasi-univalent decision

A widely-used but problematic maxim for overcoming polyvalence is the quasi-univalent decision maxim. The application has three steps:

1. First, the most important consequence type has to be determined. In the case of the apartment in Figure 8.11, this might be the rent.
2. Then minimum requirements are formulated for the other consequence types. Options that fail to meet these minimum requirements are eliminated. For example, one could fix the minimum living space at 100 m^2 and the minimum living comfort at "good". As a result, option C would be eliminated.
3. Finally, the remaining options are ordered according to the most important consequence type. This means that in the example apartment A would be chosen because it has a lower rent than apartment B.

The quasi-univalent decision maxim is simple to understand and therefore relatively popular in practice. However, there are two significant problems related to this maxim and for this reason it cannot be recommended:

- If minimum requirements must be applied to the options, they should already have been determined during problem analysis in Step 2 or when developing options in Step 3. In the apartment example, whether apartment C is an option should already have been determined in Step 2 or 3. If 90m^2 of living space and satisfactory living comfort suffices, apartment C is an option. However, if 100m^2 of living space and good living comfort are required, apartment C should not be included as an option in the decision matrix at all.
- If for the less important consequence types, no important restrictive conditions are fixed, then the decision will be made on the basis of the most important consequence type. This would be the case for example, if 90m^2 of living space and satisfactory living comfort represent the basic conditions for the two less important consequence types. In this case, one would judge the options exclusively on the basis of the rent, so that apartment C would be chosen. However, where strict additional conditions are imposed in respect of the less important consequence types, one would decide only on this basis. This would be the case if 100m^2 of living space and very good liv-

ing comfort was required. In this case both apartment A and apartment C would be dropped on the basis of these extra conditions. Apartment B would be chosen even though it rates lowest on the most important consequence type, the rent.

8.4   Decision maxims for overcoming risk

8.4.1   Expectation value maxim

As probabilities of occurrence are known for the uncertain consequence values, an obvious rule is to multiply each uncertain consequence value by its probability and to add these values for each option. The total reached in this way is called the expectation value. The option with the highest expectation value is chosen.

However, a decision on the basis of the expectation value alone is problematic. Imagine an actor who has to choose between two investment projects. The success of these projects will depend on whether the patenting of the manufactured product succeeds. **Figure 8.12** shows the consequences and expectation values for the two options. As can be seen in the illustration, based on expectation value, investment A is clearly preferable. However, if patenting is refused, project A would incur losses of 0.5 million Swiss francs, much more than project B. Losses on this scale put the continuation of the company in doubt. Thus option A will not be chosen despite its higher expectation value.

In accordance with the application conditions proposed in decision logic, expectation value is only a good decision maxim where the same decision often recurs. In these cases expectation value is not merely an average value that never actually occurs, but becomes a reference value for all decisions (Rommenfanger & Eickemeier, 2002, p. 65 ff.). From a practical point of view however, the expectation value decision maxim can be used when the individual consequences do not represent any substantial risks and are therefore judged to be bearable. This will not generally be the case with important decisions, however. Those important decisions which need the application of a formal rational decision-making procedure will typically be one-time decisions involving considerable risk.

Criteria, scenarios and probabi- lities / Options	Return in millions of Swiss francs		Probability
	Patenting possible	Patenting impossible	
	Expectation value 0.8	Expectation value 0.2	
Investment A	+ 1	- 0.5	+ 0.7
Investment B	+ 0.4	+ 0.1	+ 0.34

Figure 8.12: Example of expectation values

8.4.2   Utility expectation value

This maxim, developed by Bernoulli, requires the actor to transform the consequence values into utility values before calculating the expectation value. With this procedure, the actor's attitude to risk is taken into account (Bamberg & Coenenberg, 2002, p. 81 ff.; Bitz, 1981, p. 153 ff.; Rommelfanger & Eickemeier, 2002, p. 72 ff.). There are two steps in applying the maxim:

1. The consequence values are transformed into utility values which take into account the attitude to risk.
2. These utility values are transformed into the utility expectation values of the options, in the same way as was done for the simple expectation values.

The application of this maxim will now be illustrated in an example. An actor is offered the general agency for products from two suppliers. Since the two products are in competition with each other, he/she can only take on one of the two. **Figure 8.13** shows the contribution margin of the products in euro after the deduction of all those costs which are dependent on the decision.

Criteria, scenarios and probabi- lities / Options	Contribution margins in euro		
	Poor economic situation	Average economic situation	Good economic situation
	Probability 0.25	Probability 0.4	Probability 0.35
Product A	0	15,000,000	30,000,000
Product B	-30,000,000	15,000,000	70,000,000

Figure 8.13: Example of the utility expectation value maxim: starting point

These consequence values are now transformed into utility values. **Figure 8.14** shows the transformation curve. As can be seen from the illustration, the actor assigns utility values to the consequence values that clearly lie above the diagonal. The curve expresses a pronounced risk-averse attitude on the part of the actor: for example, the actor assigns a utility value of 0.8 to a contribution margin of 0. If the conversion of the consequence values to utility values had been risk-neutral, the contribution margin of 0 would only have had the utility value of 0.3.

Once the transformation into utility values has taken place, the utility expectation values can be calculated. **Figure 8.15** shows the calculation of these values for the two options. A cautious attitude to risk causes the actor to choose Product A. This means passing up the chance of making €70 million profit from Product B, but at the same time avoiding the risk of losing €30 million.

In the example, the consequence values have been transformed into utility values with the help of a curve. In the literature, however, it is usually recommended to carry out the transformation with a game. **Inset 8.3** explains this game, which is based on Ramsey (1931).

University of Chester, Riverside Library

Title: Successful decision making in [...]

ID: [...]
Due: 04 Jul 2019

Title: [...] decision making in health [...]

ID: [...]
Due: 04 Jul 2019

Total items: 2
13/06/2019 12:53

Renew online at
https://library.chester.ac.uk/patroninfo

Thank you for using Self Check

72

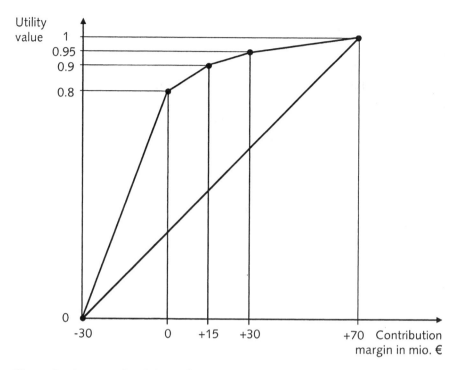

Figure 8.14: Example of the utility expectation value maxim: possible curve for the transformation of consequence values into utility values

Criteria, scenarios + probabilities	Utility values on contribution margin in euro			Utility expectation values
	Poor economic situation	Average economic situation	Good economic situation	
Options	Probability 0.25	Probability 0.4	Probability 0.35	
Product A	0.80 0.20	0.90 0.36	0.95 0.33	– 0.89
Product B	0.00 0.00	0.90 0.36	1.00 0.35	– 0.71
Upper figures = utility values Lower figures = utility values weighted according to probability				

Figure 8.15: Example of the utility expectation value maxim: calculation of the utility expectation values

Inset 8.3: Determining utility values by means of a game

There is a game which can be used to transform consequence values into utility values which reflect the attitude to risk of the actors. This is a procedure which dates back to Ramsey (1931, Bamberg & Coenenberg, 2002, p. 90; Rommelfanger & Eickemeier, 2002, p. 74).

In this game, the actor has to choose between a prize of fixed value and a lottery ticket with two possible values, one of which is higher and the other lower in value than the fixed prize. The actor is asked to specify how great the probability of occurrence of the higher value for the lottery ticket would need to be in order for the actor to regard the fixed prize and the lottery ticket as having equal value. This assessment indicates the actor's attitude to risk. The lower the risk acceptance, the greater the probability must be that the higher figure will occur if the fixed prize and the lottery ticket are to be regarded as equivalent by the actor. Conversely, a high risk tolerance of the actor means that, even with a relatively low probability for the higher prize in the lottery-draw, the lottery-ticket and the fixed prize will be seen as equivalent.

The game is played using the consequence values of the decision problem:
- In each game the higher and lower values of the lottery-draw correspond to the highest and lowest consequence values.
- The fixed prize is one of the other consequence values.

Figure 8.16 once more presents the decision matrix of our example of the maxim of the utility expectation value. This time the figure also shows how the consequence values are used in the games. In the matrix there are five different consequence values. The highest and the lowest values are always taken as the amounts for the lottery draw; they receive utility values of 1 and 0. Three games are needed to determine the utility values for the other three consequence values.

Scenarios and probabilities / Options	Poor economic situation	Average economic situation	Good economic situation
	Probability 0.25	Probability 0.4	Probability 0.35
Product A	0 Game I Prize	15,000,000 Game II Prize	30,000,000 Game III Prize
Product B	-30,000,000	15,000,000 Game II Prize	-70,000,000

Possible lottery results

Figure 8.16: The consequence values of the decision problem as starting point of the game

The game can be algebraically represented as follows:

Fixed prize $\approx$ p* • higher lottery result + (1-p*) • lower lottery result

p* corresponds to the probability for the higher amount in the lottery required by the actor so that the fixed prize and participation in the lottery are regarded as equivalent. The higher the required probability p*, the more risk-averse the actor.

In the first game, the actor must fix p* for the following situations:

$0 \approx p^* \bullet (70,000,000) + (1-p^*) \bullet (-30,000,000)$

An actor judging in the same way as in the transformation curve illustrated in Figure 8.14 would require a value of 0.8 for p* for the two options in the game to become equivalent.

If in the further two games p* is fixed at 0.9 and 0.95 respectively, the same five values will result as in the transformation curve in Figure 8.14:

$-30,000,000 \rightarrow 0$
$0 \rightarrow 0.8$
$15,000,000 \rightarrow 0.9$
$30,000,000 \rightarrow 0.95$
$70,000,000 \rightarrow 1$

⌐ These five values can now be used to calculate the utility expecta-
∟ tion values for the options in the decision problem.

Bernoulli's utility expectation value maxim is based on the assumption
that the actor is capable of expressing an attitude to risk with the help
of a transformation curve of games. Studies by Kahneman & Tversky
(1982) cast some doubt on whether this assumption is valid. They
suggest that the way the actor is questioned exerts an essential influence on the attitude to risk that is manifested. **Inset 8.4** discusses
these "framing" effects.

**Inset 8.4: Distorted recording of the attitude to risk through
framing effects**

Kahnemen and Tversky (1982) have shown empirically that the
way a problem is presented leads to different statements of attitude to risk.

Von Nitsch (2002, p. 113 ff.) shows how risk behaviour can be
manipulated in an example comparing two decision situations:

- Situation A: You get €1,000 in an envelope and must choose
  between receiving a further fixed amount of €500 or taking part
  in a game in which you will either get nothing or receive an additional €1,000, with a probability of 50% for each.
- Situation B: You get €2,000 in an envelope and must choose
  whether to hand back €500 or to take part in a game in which
  you must either hand back a further €1,000 or hand back nothing at all, with a 50% probability for each.

As **Figure 8.17** shows, both these situations invite decisions about
whether one prefers to hold on to a guaranteed sum of €1,500, or
to take part in a game which offers a 50% chance of finishing with
only €1,000 and a 50% chance of finishing with €2,000 (von
Nitsch, 2002, p. 113 ff.).

As the empirical studies of Kahneman and Tversky (1982) show,
most people will decide differently in the two situations, because

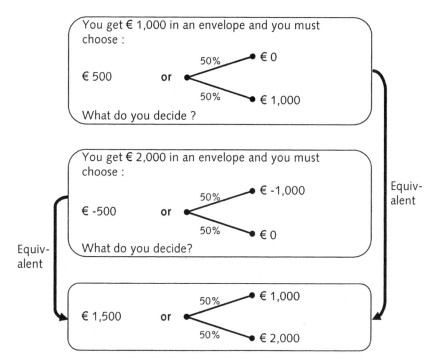

Figure 8.17: Two different representations of the same decision problem (von Nitsch, 2002, p. 113).

they are influenced by the way the situation is presented. In Situation A they will choose the guaranteed €1,500 and in Situation B they prefer the game. They do this for the following reason: the situations have two stages: a first stage with a guaranteed amount and a second stage with a game. The guaranteed amount of the first stage suggests a reference point for the second stage. In the second stage, the risks are assessed, based on the specific reference point from the first stage. In situation A, the reference point for the second step is €1,000 and the additional amounts are therefore relative gains. In situation B, the reference point is €2,000 and the risk evaluation deals with relative losses (von Nitsch, 2002, p. 114).

8.4.3   Problems with the application of the decision maxims for overcoming risk

The use of the decision-maxims proposed for overcoming risk can be problematic:

- As we have seen, the maxim of expectation value is only applicable with repetitive decisions and with less important one-time decisions with low risk. Important complex decisions are one-time decisions with risk-laden consequences. To solve these decisions it is not enough to calculate the expectation value, as this does not take the actor's attitude to risk into account.
- The utility expectation value maxim corrects this serious disadvantage of the expectation value maxim. Through the application of a transformation function or with the use of games, the actor can bring attitude to risk into the decision. However, the application of the maxim is costly and demanding, as will have been clear from the previous subsection. This may be the reason why the maxim is rarely applied in practice. Moreover the determination of the attitude to risk can be falsified by framing effects.

These difficulties can be avoided by deliberately ignoring information about probabilities and treating the decision as an uncertain problem, rather than a risky one. In practice this will often be an attractive choice, since maxims for overcoming uncertainty can then be applied, some of which are very easy to use, as will be shown in the following section. An actor who takes this decision must be conscious that information about probabilities is being left out of consideration. Attitude to risk, however, can easily be incorporated into the decision. This means that the importance of the attitude to risk is increased in the decision at the expense of the influence of factual knowledge.

8.5   Decision maxims for overcoming uncertainty

Five decision maxims are recommended for dealing with uncertain problems (Bamberg & Coenenberg, 2002, p. 129 ff.; Bitz, 1981, p. 62 ff.; Laux, 2002, p. 106 ff.; Rommelfanger & Eickemeier, 2002, p. 51 ff.):

- The minimax maxim of Wald
- the maximax maxim
- the maxim of the equal probability of Laplace
- the optimism-pessimism index of Hurwicz
- the minimax-risk maxim from Niehans and Savage

Each of these five maxims will be presented and explained with an example.

Wald's minimax maxim compares options on the basis of their worst consequences. The option which performs best among these worst consequence values is chosen. The application of the minimax rule corresponds to extreme risk-averse behaviour, or to a worst case attitude.

The maximax maxim is exactly the opposite. It requires the actor to look only at the best consequence values for each option and to go for the alternative that displays the highest value.

The rule of equal probability represents a middle course between the minimax and maximax. As its name suggests, it makes the assumption that all consequence values are equally likely. The maxim therefore provides that an average consequence value is determined for each option and that the actor then chooses the option with the best of these values.

In the same way as the maxim of equal probability, the optimism-pessimism-index seeks a middle course between the extreme provisions of the maximax and the minimax. This maxim is applied in three steps:

1. The actor fixes a value for the optimism-pessimism-index between 0 and 1. The higher the value, the more optimistic or risk-tolerant the actor is.
2. For each option, the best consequence value is multiplied by the index value and the worst consequence value is multiplied by the difference between the index value and 1.
3. For each option these two products are added. The option with the best value is chosen. The best value means the highest sum for

positive consequences and the lowest sum for negative consequences.

Niehans and Savage's minimax-risk maxim takes a different approach. Unlike the other four maxims, it does not consider the consequence values from a more or less pessimistic or optimistic viewpoint but looks at the differences between the consequence values of the different options in a scenario. If the actor decides in favour of option A and scenario 1 then follows, the actor is interested in the difference between the consequence of option A and the consequence of the optimal option in scenario 1. If this difference is great, this means a correspondingly great regret. If the difference is small, the actor's regret is smaller. If the best option for the occurring scenario was chosen, then there is no regret. The minimax-risk maxim tries to minimize the regret as much as possible. There are three steps:

1. For each scenario the differences between the best consequence value and the other values are calculated. They represent possible regrets in the various scenarios.
2. The highest possible regret for each option is identified.
3. The actor decides in favour of the option where the highest possible regret is the lowest.

The five maxims will now be illustrated in an example. An actor is given the general agency for products offered by three suppliers. Since the products are in competition with each other, only one of them can be included in his product range. **Figure 8.18** shows the contribution margins of each product after the deduction of all costs dependent on the decision.

According to the minimax maxim, product A must be chosen. The zero figure for option A is the best of the lowest consequence values for the three options.

If the maximax rule is used, then Product B will be preferred. The € 70 million contribution margin represents the highest consequence value.

According to the maxim of equal probability, the average consequences have to be calculated for all three options. They amount to:

Criteria, scenarios / Options	Total contribution margin in millions of euro		
	Poor economic situation	Average economic situation	Good economic situation
Product A	0	15	30
Product B	- 30	15	70
Product C	- 10	10	60

Figure 8.18: Starting point for the illustration of use of the maxims for overcoming uncertainty

- € 15 million for option A,
- € 18.333 million for option B
- € 20 million for option C.

According to this maxim product C should be chosen.

If we use the optimism-pessimism-index maxim, the result will depend on the optimism or risk-acceptance of the actor. An index-value of $1/3$ means that the actor is pessimistic or cautious. With this assumption, the following overall consequences are produced for the three options:

- $1/3$ • € 30 m. + $2/3$ • € 0 = € 10 m. for option A
- $1/3$ • € 70 m. + $2/3$ • € (-30) m.= € 3.333 m. for option B
- $1/3$ • € 60 m. + $2/3$ • € (-10) m.= € 13.333 m. for option C

Here option C is chosen.

Figure 8.19 shows the result of the application of the minimax-risk maxim. As can be seen from the illustration, the maximum disappointment is the lowest with option C. This option is therefore the one to choose.

Criteria and scenarios / Options	Total contribution margin in millions of euro			Maximum regret
	Poor economic situation	Average eco- nomic situation	Good eco- nomic situation	
Product A	0 - 0 = 0	15 - 15 = 0	70 - 30 = 40	40
Product B	0 - (-30) = 30	15 - 15 = 0	70 - 70 = 0	30
Product C	0 - (-10) = 10	15 - 10 = 5	70 - 60 = 10	10

Figure 8.19: Application of the minimax-risk maxim

8.6   Using decision maxims in combination to overcome polyvalence and risk or polyvalence and uncertainty

If polyvalence and risk or polyvalence and uncertainty are simultaneously present, two maxims must be applied for the determination of the overall consequences, one after the other. Although this introduces no new methodical problems, it does complicate the determination of the overall consequences. Inset 8.5 shows the determination of the overall consequences in a decision problem with polyvalence and uncertainty and therefore the combined application of two maxims.

Inset 8.5: Determining the overall consequences in a polyvalent and uncertain decision problem

The decision problem in which polyvalence and uncertainty have to be overcome simultaneously is already known to our readers: It relates to the family business which wants to extend its operations geographically and wants to enter the German and Polish markets. Since the company is owned by a Polish family, when evaluating the four options the creation of jobs in Poland is included as a decision criterion, together with discounted cash flow. The discounted cash flow figures of the options will depend on how well the integration of the new activities succeeds and how many positive synergies can be created.

Figure 8.20 shows the decision matrix.

Criteria and scenarios	C_1: Discounted cash flow of the next 5 years in millions of euro		C_2: Creation of jobs in Poland (*)
Options	S_1: Integration goes well	S_2: Integration goes badly	
O_1: Buy manufacturer U with production plants in Germany and Poland	$c_{111} = 10$	$c_{112} = -4$	$c_{12} =$ many
O_2: Buy manufacturer V with a production plant in Poland and sales agencies in Germany	$c_{211} = 5$	$c_{212} = -2$	$c_{22} =$ very many
O_3: Create new sales agencies in Germany and Poland for products from Switzerland	$c_{311} = 2$	$c_{312} = 0$	$C_{32} =$ few
O_4: No expansion	$c_{41} = 0$		$c_{42} =$ none

O_x = Options
C_y = Criteria
S_z = Scenarios
c_{xy} = Single consequence of option x in relation to criterion y
c_{xyz} = Single consequence of option x in relation to criterion y and scenario z
(*) Measure on the ordinal scale with the categories "very many", "many", "some", "few" and "none"

Figure 8.20: Decision matrix as starting point

Starting from the decision matrix, uncertainty is first overcome with the help of the equal probability maxim. The application of this maxim is a risk-neutral approach and is justifiable because the company can accept a discounted cash drain of four million euro. **Figure 8.21** shows the result.

Criteria and scenarios / Options	C_1: Discounted cash flow of the next 5 years in millions of euro	C_2: Creation of jobs in Poland (*)
O_1: Buy manufacturer U with production plants in Germany and Poland	$c_{11} = 3$	c_{12} = many
O_2: Buy manufacturer V with a production plant in Poland and sales agencies in Germany	$c_{21} = 1.5$	c_{22} = very many
O_3: Create new sales agencies in Germany and Poland for products from Switzerland	$c_{31} = 1$	c_{32} = few
O_4: No expansion	$c_{41} = 0$	c_{42} = none

O_x = Options
C_y = Criteria
c_{xy} = Single consequence of option x in relation to criterion y
(*) Measure on the ordinal scale with the categories "very many", "many", "some", "few" and "none"

Figure 8.21: Decision matrix after overcoming uncertainty

Criteria and scenarios	C₁: Discounted cash flow of the next 5 years in millions of euro	C₂: Creation of jobs in Poland (*)	Overall consequences
Options	W₁: 0.67	W₂: 0.33	
O₁: Buy manufacturer U with production plants in Germany and Poland	0.545 0.365	0.333 0.110	- 0.475
O₂: Buy manufacturer V with a production plant in Poland and sales agencies in Germany	0.273 0.183	0.417 0.138	- 0.321
O₃: Create new sales agencies in Germany and Poland for products from Switzerland	0.182 0.122	0.167 0.055	- 0.177
O₄: No expansion	0.000 0.000	0.083 0.027	- 0.027
Total	1.000 0.330	1.000 0.330	1.000 0.330

Oₓ = Options
C_y = Criteria
W_z = Weights
Upper figures = utility values
Lower figures = weighted utility values
(*) Measure on the ordinal scale with the categories "very many", "many", "some", "few" and "none"

Figure 8.22: Decision matrix after overcoming polyvalence

Next, the consequence values are transformed into utility values. The discounted cash flow is weighted at 0.67 and the creation of jobs in Poland is weighted at 0.33. **Figure 8.22** shows the utility values, the weighted utility values and the overall consequences of the four options. As can be seen from the illustration, option O_1 attains the highest total utility value by a clear distance. It is therefore the one to be chosen although it carries the highest risk.

8.7   Evaluation of the decision maxims

After discussing the advantages and disadvantages of the individual maxims in the sections 8.3 to 8.6 we now present a systematic evaluation. **Figure 8.24** shows the scope of application, the application costs and the strengths and weaknesses of the different decision maxims.

Most of the information in Figure 8.24 is familiar from the above sections 8.3 to 8.6. However, the bottom right hand field of the diagram includes the statement that for each maxim used to overcome uncertainty, there are decision situations where the use of the maxim will lead to a rather implausible result. **Figure 8.23** presents a decision situation in which even a risk-averse actor should not decide according to the minimax maxim. Even if nothing is known about the probabilities, here it is hardly sensible to pass up the opportunities for profit represented by option A in four of the five scenarios because the worst case is 1% worse for option A than for option B (Krelle, 1968, p. 185; Rommelfanger & Eickemeier, 2002, p. 51 ff.).

Scenarios Options	Scenario 1	Scenario 2	Scenario 3	Scenario 4	Scenario 5
Option A	0.99	10	10	10	10
Option B	1	1	1	1	1

Figure 8.23: Example of a decision situation in which the minimax maxim should not be applied
(adapted from Krelle, 1968, p. 185)

Decision maxim	Application area	Application expenditure	Strengths	Weaknesses/Problems
Utility value	Overcoming polyvalence	significant	Allows a correct summary of different consequences into overall consequences	—
Quasi-univalent decision		limited	—	▪ Establishing levels of requirements should be part of the problem analysis or of the development of options and should not be part of establishing the overall consequences ▪ Depending on the levels of requirements, the less important consequence types may have too great significance
Expectation value	Overcoming risk	limited	—	▪ Does not consider the actor's attitude to risk ▪ Is therefore only suitable for repeated, similar decisions or for low-risk decisions
Utility expectation value		significant	Allows attitude to risk to be incorporated into risk decisions	▪ Establishing the actor's attitude to risk ▪ Framing effects can distort the attitude to risk
Minimax Maximax Equal probability	Overcoming uncertainty	limited	By means of the selection of the decision maxim, the attitude to risk can be considered in uncertain decision	▪ For risk problems, information regarding the probabilities of the different scenarios is left out of consideration ▪ There are decision situations in which the application can lead to rather implausible decisions
Optimism-peptimism-index		middling		
Minimax risk				

Figure 8.24: Evaluation of different decision maxims

9 A case study illustrating the application of the procedure

9.1 The situation

SV is a manufacturer of specialist vehicles for use in forestry and for the upkeep of road embankments, sporting fields and golf courses. The company is based in the east of Switzerland. Most of the vehicles are sold in Germany, Austria and Switzerland by the company's own representatives in the field. For the last two years, the products have also been distributed by representatives in France, Belgium and Italy. Until now success has been modest.

Four years ago SV acquired a supplier in difficulty, a Zurich-based producer of chassis for utility vehicles. The Zurich company continues to supply other Swiss utility vehicle makers alongside SV.

Figure 9.1 shows the organigram of the group, with 600 employees. As is clear from the illustration, the company had a functional structure up to the takeover of the chassis company. After the takeover, only three of the divisions of the acquired company were merged into this functional structure - development, accounting and HRM. Since then SV has been divided into six divisions which at the second level in the hierarchy include both functions and product groups.

Last year SV reported an unconsolidated turnover of approximately 310 million Swiss francs. In comparison, pre-tax profit was slight last year, at around 1 million Swiss francs.

SV is owned by the Keller and Strehl families. It is the policy of the two families that no member of the family should participate in the running of the company. For several years, the company has been managed by the economist Dr. Fritz Herren, who enjoys the full confidence of the owners and has wide-ranging executive powers.

In the problem we shall now describe, legally speaking, it is the board

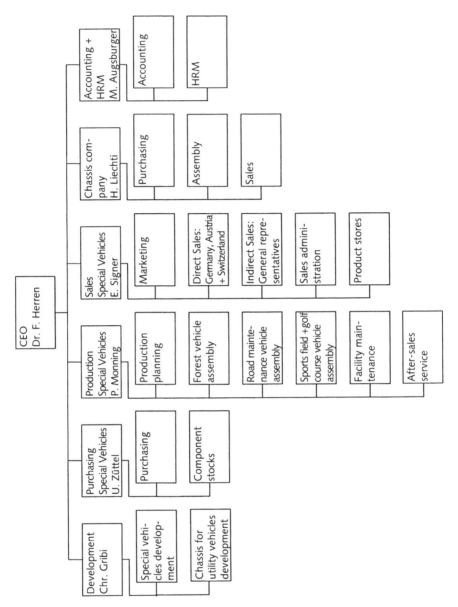

Figure 9.1: Organigram at Special Vehicles

which must take the decision. However, Dr. Herren is the de facto decision maker. The other members of the management team will actively support him in the problem analysis and in the development and evaluation of options, but he alone is responsible to the board.

Accordingly the decision-making authority falls to him, so that he is the actor for this decision.

9.2   Discovering and analysing the problem

9.2.1   Discovering the problem

At the end of February 2005, Dr. Herren receives the figures for the previous year's profit and immediately realizes that it is well below the expectations the Keller and Strehl families have for SV. From the sales figures and the half-year results to the end of June, Fritz Herren had already anticipated that 2004 would not turn out well. However, on the basis of the half-yearly results, he had calculated a profit of approximately 3.5 m. Swiss francs, a fall of 1m as against the previous year.

Herren knows that the owners, the third generation of the family who hold the majority of the shares, expect a level of earnings on their capital resources which is at least as good as that available from a low-risk bond and share portfolio. Cautious estimates put the equity capital of SV at 60 million Swiss francs. Interest of 5% from a conservative portfolio would yield 3 million francs - the level of return required by the stockholders. The company's dividend payments are further reduced because the company must of course pay tax on its profits, as well as using profits to boost its capital resources.

Based on this, it is more than clear to Dr. Herren that there is a significant discrepancy between the current situation and the target situation. If we are to speak of a decision problem, then it must be established that the discrepancy observed is derived from reliable data. When Margaret Augsburger meets him to disclose the provisional year 2004 results, Dr Herren asks her whether it is likely that these figures will need to be corrected to any significant extent. She answers as follows:

- Dr. Herren would not have been given these figures if any significant modifications had been expected.

- Because stocks were lower than expected (see subsection 9.2.2), the inventory was checked twice. The valuation of the merchandise was also double-checked. There were only slight differences, so that the figures for the value of the stock held should be treated as reliable.
- All products sold in the last year were invoiced. Expenditures for which no bills had yet arrived were provisionally entered in the books. In this way it was possible to estimate costs.
- Deductions for social insurance and value added tax had been completed in accordance with directives. For this reason, even if the authorities were to carry out an audit, Augsburger did not expect that there would be any great discrepancy.
- To sum up, in Augsburger's view, the examination of the year's results by the auditor, scheduled to take place in March, could not produce a change in the profit figure of the order of more than half a million Swiss francs.

Dr. Herren has known Margaret Augsburger for many years and she has always been a reliable colleague. He therefore has confidence in her report of the situation and concludes that the annual result is, in fact, a poor one.

The final step in this problem discovery is for Herren to determine whether or not it is economically worthwhile to embark on the treatment of the problem. In the present case, this step is purely academic. The problem is certainly significant enough to justify thorough analysis.

9.2.2 Analysing the problem

Problem analysis begins in the discussion Augsburger has with her superior about the poor results. She mentions two unusual facts:

- The chassis company had components in stock for chassis types that are no longer being produced. Their amortization represented an unforeseen expenditure of 0.45 million Swiss francs.
- The stocks of components for the special vehicles were down by 2.8 million in 2004. Augsburger asked Mr. Züttel, the purchasing manager, about this before her meeting with Herren. Züttel ex-

plained that the stock reduction was a reaction to hefty price increases for motors and driveshafts. As he is hoping that the suppliers will have to reverse these price increases, at least to some extent, he has reduced stocks to the absolute minimum.

Herren and Augsburger are able to establish that this one-time deduction from the value of the stocks held by the chassis company has helped to produce a poor annual result. However, this loss is responsible for just 0.45 million Swiss francs, only part of the shortfall against what was expected and what had been achieved in the previous year's results. Unlike the amount that had to be written off for the chassis company, the stock reduction Züttel ordered in the parent company has no effect on the year-end result. Since vehicle components are drawn from the stock on the first-in-first-out principle, the same material expenses would also have arisen without the stock reduction.

The first discussion between Augsburger and Herren closes with an agreement to meet again the following morning. In the meantime the CEO will give careful consideration to what further action to take.

The second meeting is very short and produces the following decisions:
- In a change from existing practice, cost analysis will be produced before the accounts are audited.
- In order to complete the cost analysis quickly, Dr. Herren's personal assistant will assist Augsburger. The assistant, Peter Walther, will not only speed up the process but also make sure that fixed costs are not distributed in an inappropriate way.
- This cost analysis will then be discussed by management to identify the problem causes and generate initial ideas for measures.

Figure 9.2 shows the result of a week of intensive work. Unlike earlier analysis, these new calculations do not distribute fixed costs in an inappropriate way on the cost carriers. This is what Dr Herren had wanted to achieve.

	Forest vehicles	Embank-ment vehicles	Sports field + golf course maintenance vehicles	Utility vehicle chassis
Units sold	1,100 1,050	1,900 1,900	500 450	6,800 7,600
Net sales price	82 81	67 66	37 41	10 11
Turnover	90,200 85,050	127,300 125,400	18,500 18,450	71,400 83,600
Variable production costs per unit	61 60	59 58	35 35	10 10
Variable production costs	67,100 63,525	112,100 110,200	17,500 15,750	68,000 76,000
Contribution margin I	23,100 21,525	15,200 15,200	1,000 2,700	3,400 7,600
Depreciation + Interest (*)	1,300 1,300	1,700 1,700	3,400 3,400	— —
Fixed production cost	1,100 1,100	1,000 1,000	800 725	— —
Contribution margin II	20,700 19,125	12,500 12,500	-3,200 -1,425	3,400 7,600

Figure 9.2: Cost carrier analysis

	Forest vehicles	Embank-ment vehicles	Sports field + golf course maintenance vehicles	Utility vehicle chassis
Depreciation + Interest (*)		1,100 1,100		4,000 4,000
Fixed production cost		800 800		2,000 2,200
Extraordinary depreciations in the stock		— —		450 —
Marketing and sales costs		11,650 11,650		1,600 2,350
Contribution margin III		16,650 16,350		- 4,650 - 950
Depreciation+ Interest (*)		500 500		
Development, purchas-ing, accounting, HRM and management		13,500 13,400		
Profit or loss		- 2,000 1,500		

First figure is for year 2004
Second figure is for year 2003
All figures are in thousands of Swiss francs

(*)3 million interest on the equity capital is included in the depreciations and interest totalling 12 million Swiss francs

The management session begins with the presentation of the cost analysis by Augsburger and the management assistant Walther. Hans Liechti asks whether the interest on the equity capital calculated at 3 million francs is truly necessary. Herren assures him that this amount represents an absolute minimum. A careful estimate of the equity capital puts the figure at 60 million francs and an interest rate of 5% was applied, which is less than the average interest rate of bond and share portfolios.

After the presentation, Herren opens the discussion about the causes of the problem. He decides that the meeting should not only address the causes of the deterioration in relation to the previous year but also the generally unsatisfactory profit situation. In Herren's view the downward trend began last year and does not stem from any short-term unfavourable conditions or sudden problems.

In order to structure the discussion, Dr. Herren suggests first reviewing the chassis construction. He asks Liechti to outline his view first:

- Hans Liechti apologises for the fact that the obsolete and worthless parts had not been identified in the inventory for 2003. He had taken over from the former owners only a few months before this inventory, and was not yet on top of the situation at that time.
- Next Liechti turnes to capacity utilization: the company's capacity of 10,000 chassis per year was partly utilized by the parent company, which consumed 33% of this. A further 33% could be sold to third parties. The remaining 32% is lost. Liechti had made some price reductions and the parent company had taken up 100 extra units, but total output was down about 800 units on the previous year, a drop of 8%.
- After this Liechti addresses market position. The chassis company sells two types of chassis. First, chassis are manufactured for special vehicles. Although the company offers competitive products, since the takeover many customers in this sub-market have been lost. Obviously, companies do not want to buy components from a competitor. In the last year the chassis company only had two customers besides its parent company, a fire engine maker and a producer of ambulances. Both of these take relatively small numbers of units; however they pay a good price. In addition, the chassis company produces trailer chassis. Despite offering discounts, it has lost

market share massively in this sub-market in the last year. An Asian manufacturer has been operating in the German-language area for two years with great success. As the sales figures show, the price reductions had not been significant enough to enable the company to hold on to customers.

- Finally, Hans Liechti speaks about the prices which the parent company pays for their chassis. He maintains that these prices are at least 10% below the market price. This is, however, strongly contested by Züttel, who believes that the amounts he pays are above the market rate.
- Dr. Herren interrupts this disagreement about prices and asks Liechti for suggestions for improvement. Liechti suggests that additional investment could improve productivity and reduce variable costs. This would create the conditions in which prices could be brought down to win back market share.
- At this point Züttel points out that the parent company should also be able to profit from lower market prices. Here Dr. Herren intervenes to put a stop to any further discussion of internal prices.
- Margaret Augsburger does not believe that new investment is the right way. Besides an equity capital of 45 million in the balance sheet (the effective equity capital is 60 million), the group has debts of 65 million francs. Debt capacity has already been exceeded; the banks have been demanding substantial reductions of the credits for years. The poor results for 2004 will certainly increase the pressure from the banks. The company's worsened credit rating will also increase interest rates.
- Hans Liechti responds to these comments by saying that he only wanted to indicate the basic options. He sees a second possibility in concentrating on special-vehicle chassis. But this would mean a one-time depreciation next year on parts of the capital assets.

Dr. Herren thanks Liechti for his analysis and initial proposals and moves on to the second issue, vehicles for the maintenance of sports fields and golf courses:

- When the decision was made three years ago to enter this sub-market, 750 and 1,500 units were budgeted for the years 2003 and 2004 respectively. Only 450 and 500 units were actually sold. This result is very disappointing for Dr. Herren. After these introductory remarks, he asks Eric Signer for an analysis of the market.

- Signer begins by explaining the differences from the other two categories of vehicles produced. While the forest and embankment vehicles must satisfy stringent requirements regarding all-terrain suitability and security, this does not apply to sports field and golf course vehicles. The number and type of functions that the vehicles have are also different: with forest and embankment vehicles, customers generally have high expectations and many of them ask for extra specifications. The requirements for sports field and golf course vehicles are essentially more modest and most customers are content with the standard equipment.
- The market for sports field and golf course vehicles is growing strongly in units and this trend should continue for a long time. But high competition has led to falling prices and market growth in currency has turned out to be slight. Despite lowering its prices in the last year by about 10%, the company can barely hold its market share. This shows how strong the competition is.
- The main competition does not come from other manufacturers of special vehicles but from producers of garden machines. Their products are more simply built and resemble large lawnmowers rather than vehicles. Mr. Signer says this type of competition was simply overlooked by the company when it decided to enter this market.
- Now Herren asks Gribi and Monning for their comments. Christoph Gribi points out that their sports field and golf course vehicles are a qualitatively superior product. In contrast to the "oversized lawnmowers" of the competitors, the susceptibility of the SV vehicles to repair is small, even with intensive use, and they have a long life span. Monning stresses disastrous underutilization of the assembly equipment. The capacity of 3,000 units is only being used to 16%. If the equipment were used to full capacity, a contribution margin of 2 million francs could be achieved with a reduced average price of 37,000 francs.
- Here Signer interrupts and repeats that not one single vehicle can now be sold with a price tag of 37,000 francs.

Before the session breaks for lunch, Dr. Herren asks for an assessment of how the market is developing for the other two vehicle groups and how things stand in these two areas in relation to capacity utilization:

- Signer believes that the market for forest vehicles will grow further in the medium term. Long term, he envisages either a stagnating or weakly growing market according to the degree of recognition that 'natural' forest management is able to achieve. For embankment vehicles, he foresees a long-term growing market. Since considerable accident risks exist in forests and on embankments and the public sector, which is the main employer, will not want to take any risks in these areas, Signer assumes that low-cost suppliers will find it difficult in future.
- The statement by Monning also makes the participants somewhat more positive before the lunch break. Capacity utilization for forest vehicles in 2004 was over 90%. In the same period it amounted to more than 100% for embankment vehicles. Despite overtime and temporary use of employees from the sport and golf vehicles department, delivery times for certain models were still several months. Signer adds that, given the large number of orders coming in, no potential new clients were being visited by sales representatives.

After lunch, Dr. Herren will summarize the problem analysis, undertake the problem naming and decide on further work.

9.2.3   Summary of analysis and naming the problem

The second part of the session begins with Dr. Herren explaining the causes for the unsatisfactory results with a chart on the whiteboard (see **Figure 9.3**). He is conscious that the chart includes both absolute statements and trend statements. But he claims that this does not matter as both approaches identify the same three problems:

- The group has a problem with its product portfolio: there are two cash cows with future in the portfolio, but trailer chassis and sports field and golf course vehicles are both losing money. For special vehicle chassis the situation remains unclear.
- The partially overburdened and the partially catastrophically underused production capacities, together with the necessity for a realignment of the product portfolio, indicate an investment and disinvestment problem in the area of production.

- A funding problem is clear from the high rate of credit financing, the poor annual results and possible investment needs.

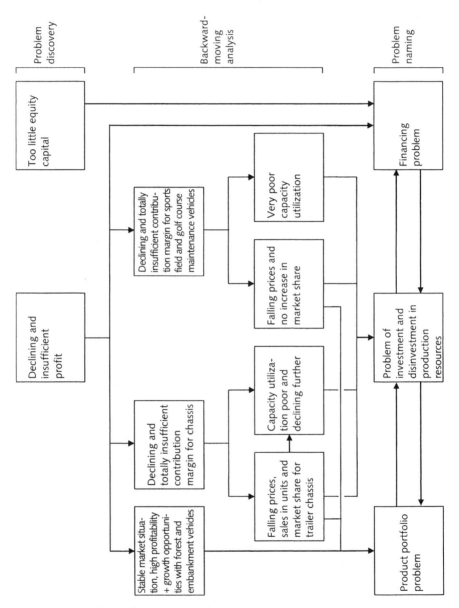

Figure 9.3: Backward-moving analysis

The possibilities and limits of possible funding will impose limits on what can be done to refocus the product portfolio and production facilities. This leads Dr. Herren to the conclusion that all three problems must be attacked simultaneously.

The management meeting agrees that the CEO's analysis of the problem is complete and accurate. Mr. Walther asks whether the company could consider raising money by issuing more shares. Dr. Herren believes that this is not really an option but he promises to speak with the family representatives about it.

At the end of the meeting Dr. Herren allocates tasks for further work:
- Augsburger and Walther will prepare figures which show how chassis construction breaks down for the three cost carriers: trailer chassis, ambulance and fire engine chassis and in-house chassis.
- Each member of the team will try to come up with possible measures. These will be combined into options at the next session.
- Herren and Augsburger will together inform the board about the results for the year 2004 and the subsequent problem analysis.

The next session will take place in four days' time.

9.3   Developing and evaluating options

9.3.1   Developing options

At the next management session Dr. Herren first informs the group about the extraordinary board meeting. He refrains from repeating any of their emotional comments. Two facts must be reported:
- The Keller and Strehl families rule out a share issue and will not provide any new capital themselves.
- The board expects proposals for stringent measures to ensure a rapid and lasting improvement in profit performance.

Dr. Herren now asks Augsburger and Walther to present their conclusions regarding the profitability of the different chassis types. Mr.

Walther distributes a summary (see **Figure 9.4**) and adds the following comments:

- Since all products are based on the same production and sales infrastructure, an attribution of the fixed costs was unnecessary. As a result only the figures for the Contribution margin I have been broken down for the different product types. Additionally, it can be assumed that the marketing and sales expenses of 1.6 million Swiss francs must be ascribed mainly to the products which are not sold on internally.
- The figures for the Contribution margin I are estimates rather than exact calculations. Since it was not possible to determine the values

	Chassis for the company's own forest and embankment vehicles	Chassis for the company's own sports field and golf course vehicles	Chassis for ambulances and fire engines	Trailer chassis	Total
Units sold	3,000	500	900	2,400	6,800
Net sales price	13.1	6	19	5	10.5
Turnover	39,300	3,000	17,100	12,000	71,400
Variable production costs per unit	12.4	6.2	16	5,542	10
Variable production costs	37,200	3,100	14,400	13,300	68,000
Contribution margin I	2,100	-100	2,700	-1,300	3,400

All figures are in thousands of Swiss francs

Figure 9.4: Contribution margin I for the four cost carriers of the chassis company for the year 2004

for 2003, the table only shows the year 2004. As considerable quality and price differences exist between chassis for forest and embankment vehicles on the one hand and chassis for sports field and golf course vehicles on the other hand, they decided to go beyond their initial brief and divide the company's own products into two different cost carriers.

- Augsburger and Walther consider that the prices fixed by the parent company are justified. They are close to the market price. However, by not using outside suppliers, the company makes cost savings with respect to quality control of incoming merchandise and in the procurement of spare parts.
- The contribution margin calculation indicates that trailer chassis production must be halted at once.

Nobody disputes Mr. Walther's conclusions. Dr. Herren moves on to the next point for discussion and asks each member of the team to present their ideas for a way to move forward:

- Margaret Augsburger begins with a radical suggestion. The production of utility vehicle chassis and sports field and golf course vehicle chassis will be shut down and the assets sold at the best price available. The premises of the chassis company are situated in the Greater Zurich area and should bring in considerable revenue.
- Peter Monning agrees that the chassis company should close. But he would like to convert the sports field and golf course vehicle production lines for the production of embankment vehicles. Urs Züttel supports him on this and emphasizes once again that he can obtain chassis from other suppliers at the same prices offered by the group's chassis company.
- Christoph Gribi is next to speak. He observes that the chassis are at present an important component of the forest and embankment vehicles. They are essential for their stability and safety. He would therefore regret losing chassis construction skills and suggests moving chassis construction to the parent company and giving up the production of sports field and golf course maintenance vehicles. This would make it possible to sell the Zurich property. Hans Liechti comments that this is a good idea. But he also points out that if the company limits itself to producing high-price chassis this will not mean any reduction in fixed production costs in the chassis company.

- Dr. Herren raises the question of whether to introduce a double-shift system for the production of embankment vehicles. This would mean that demand could be met fully without any new investment, realizing a considerable increase in contribution margin. Augsburger supports this, adding that workers for the new shift could be drawn from employees laid off by the ending of production of the sports and golf vehicles.
- Finally, Hans Liechti suggests appointing a new sales representative to find new clients for chassis, perhaps firms constructing small field trucks for military use. Dr. Herren comments that it is a pity that this had not been tried earlier.

Since no further proposals are forthcoming, Dr. Herren attempts to summarize the ideas by creating options. **Figure 9.5** shows the outcome of an hour at the whiteboard. As can be seen from the matrix, five options have emerged:

- Option 1a is based on Augsburger's suggestion. Her response to the problem of chassis production and sports and golf vehicle production is radical disinvestment to reduce the company's debt.
- Option 1b combines Augsburger's proposition with that of Dr. Herren. Creating two shifts for the production of the embankment vehicles would make it possible to take advantage of market opportunities at the same time as realizing the benefits of disinvestment.
- Option 2 has been developed from Monning's proposal. Facilities used up to now for the construction of sports and golf maintenance vehicles would be converted to the production of embankment vehicles. As for chassis building, the unprofitable products would be dropped in favour of chassis with an attractive contribution.
- Option 3a, based on Gribi's suggestion, involves getting rid of the Zurich property as well as closing production of unprofitable products.
- Option 3b envisages introducing double shifts for the production of embankment vehicles in addition to what is proposed in option 3a.

		1a Radical disinvestment	1b Radical disinvestment and double-shift production	2 Abandon unprofitable products	3a Abandon unprofitable products and sell the Zurich plant	3b Abandon unprofitable products, sell the Zurich plant and double-shift production
Chassis company	Close production of trailer chassis			X	X	X
	Close down entirely and disinvest	X	X			
	Transfer special chassis construction to parent company and dispose of plant				X	X
	Find new clients for special chassis			X	X	X
Special vehicle company	Close production of sport and golf vehicles and sell equipment	X	X		X	X
	Close production of sports and golf vehicles and use the equipment to produce embankment vehicles			X		
	Introduce double shifts for production of embankment vehicles		X			X

Figure 9.5: The five options

9.3.2 Evaluating options

Dr. Herren is pleased with the five options and would now like to move the decision-making process forward swiftly to a result. To do this, he plans to establish decision criteria and to organize the evaluation of the options at once, even though this was not originally on the agenda for the meeting.

Dr. Herren proposes the first three decision criteria himself. These are the changes in the annual results, the investments and the disinvestments that each option would mean. Augsburger adds the number of expected redundancies as a decision criterion. Signer proposes the change in market position and Gribi suggests changes in know-how.

No one objects to any of these criteria. Herren thinks that it can be assumed that these criteria are largely independent of each other and therefore decides to use them to assess the five options. The effects of the options on the result and the needed investments and disinvestments will be determined by Augsburger in cooperation with Signer, Monning and Liechti. Walther will again help with working out the numbers. Redundancies are to be determined by Manning and Liechti. The remaining two criteria will be assessed by the whole management team, led by Signer and Gribi.

It is clear that the consequences of the options are partly uncertain. The potential revenues from the sale of production facilities and the extent to which additional orders can be secured both seem especially difficult to estimate. Because it seems impossible to allocate probabilities for the consequence values, the decision problem is subject to uncertainty. In consideration of the difficult situation in which the company finds itself, only a worst case view is acceptable for Dr. Herren. He therefore orders that only pessimistic values will be determined.

The next session is scheduled to take place three days later.

At the start of the session, Augsburger and Walther distribute a detailed table showing financial effects for each option (see **Figure 9.6**). They explain each figure in turn. Afterwards Dr. Herren asks two questions:

- Are the sales increase forecasts of around 400 embankment vehicles and 300 special chassis attainable under unfavourable conditions? Signer and Liechti confirm that they consider these numbers represent the most pessimistic targets.
- Are the figures for disinvestment realistic? Augsburger answers that if the sale of the Zurich property is not urgent and can be delayed for up to two years, she considers 20 million Swiss francs an

	Profit improvements	Investment	Disinvestment
1a Radical disin-vestment	• 3 million from discontinuation of sports and golf vehicles • 3.1 million from discontinuation of chassis construction, from the negative contribution margin III only the depreciations will remain • 1.5 million interest savings as a result of disinvestment	—	• 20 million property sale • 6 million chassis construction equipment • 4 million sports and golf vehicle assembly equipment
1b Radical disin-vestment and dou-ble-shift produc-tion	• 3 million from discontinuation of sports and golf vehicles • 3.1 million from discontinuation of chassis construction, from the negative contribution margin III only the depreciations will remain • 2 million additional contribution margin from 400 embankment vehicles, the supplementary costs of the double-shift taken into consideration • 1.5 million interest savings as a result of disinvestment	—	• 20 million property sale. • 6 million chassis construction equipment • 4 million sports and golf vehicle assembly equipment
2 Abandon un profit-able products	• 3 million from discontinuation of sports and golf vehicles • 1.2 million from discontinuation of trailer chassis and chassis from sports and golf vehicles • 3 million additional contribution margin from 400 embankment vehicles • 0.2 million additional contribution margin from 400 embankment vehicles • 0.9 million additional contribution margin from 800 additional special chassis for third parties • -0.8 million interest payments and depreciations on new investment	4 million for conversion of sports and golf vehicles facilities	—
3a Abandon unprofit-able products and sell the Zurich plant	• 3 million from discontinuation of sports and golf vehicles • 1.2 million from discontinuation of trailer chassis and chassis for sports and golf vehicles • 0.9 million additional contribution on 300 special chassis for third parties • -1 million interest payments and depreciations on new investments • 1.2 million interest savings from disinvestment	5 million for moving the chassis construction facilities	• 20 million property sale • 4 million sports and golf vehicle assembly equipment
3b Abandon unprofit-able products, sell the Zurich plant and double-shift pro-duction	• 3 million from discontinuation of sports and golf vehicles • 1.2 million from discontinuation of trailer chassis and chassis for sports and golf vehicles • 2 million additional contribution for 400 embankment vehicles, the supplementary costs of the double-shift taken into consid-eration. • 0.2 million additional contribution margin for 400 chassis for embankment vehicles • -1 million interest payments and depreciations on new investments • 1.2 million interest savings from disinvestment	5 million for moving the chassis construction facilities	• 20 million property sale • 4 million sports and golf vehicle assembly equipment

Figure 9.6: The financial effects of the five options

absolute minimum. As for the value of the production facilities, here Liechti and Monning are more equivocal: although the stated values are well below the utility value, a company would first have to be found which would be interested in these assembly facilities. Potential buyers might be sought in the countries of the former Soviet Union, although there is no direct contact with these countries at present. When he hears their answer Dr. Herren halves the figures for the proceeds of selling these facilities and for the corresponding savings in interest payments.

Next the team turns to the consequences of the options in the market. Here, a table worked out by Signer is the basis for the discussion (see **Figure 9.7**). After a brief review, the team determines that the table is complete and accurate.

The consequence matrix is now outlined on the whiteboard. **Figure 9.8** shows the result of this work which will form the basis for the final decision.

9.4   Making the decision

After examining the decision matrix reproduced in Figure 9.8, it is clear to Dr. Herren that he will propose option 3b to the board.

The main considerations are the following:

- The company's financial situation means that any option which will not bring a substantial easing of the debt is problematic. The company's poor results will increase the pressure from the banks and financing loans from private individuals is very expensive. For these reasons option 2 is not realizable.
- Since the introduction of shifts promises an additional 2 million Swiss francs contribution margin from embankment vehicles, this option must be realized. Options 1a and 3a are therefore not considered further.

	Change in market position
1a Radical disin-vestment	• Get out of the chassis market • Get out of the sports and golf vehicles sub-market - it is price sensitive and doesn't suit resources • Maintain a strong position in the attractive forest and embankment vehicle sub-markets
1b Radical disin-vestment and double-shift produc-tion	• Get out of the chassis market • Get out of the sports and golf vehicles sub-market - it is price sensitive and doesn't suit resources • Reinforce the already strong position in the attractive embankment vehicles sub-market, maintain a strong position in the attractive forest-vehicle sub-market
2 Abandon unprofit-able products	• Concentrate chassis construction on the special vehicle chassis sub-market which is attractive, fits resources and creates synergies with vehicle construc-tion • Get out of the sports and golf vehicles sub-market - it is price sensitive and doesn't suit resources • Reinforce the already strong position in the attractive embankment vehicles sub-market, maintain a strong position in the attractive forest-vehicle sub-market
3a Abandon unprofit-able products and sell the Zu-rich plant	• Concentrate chassis construction on the special vehicle chassis sub-market which is attractive, fits resources and creates synergies with vehicle construc-tion • Get out of the sports and golf vehicles sub-market - it is price sensitive and doesn't suit resources • Maintain a strong position in the attractive forest-vehicle sub-market
3b Abandon unprofit-able products, sell the Zurich plant + double-shift pro-duction	• Concentrate chassis construction on the special vehicle chassis sub-market which is attractive, fits resources and creates synergies with vehicle construc-tion • Get out of the sports and golf vehicles sub-market - it is price sensitive and doesn't suit resources • Reinforce the already strong position in the attractive embankment vehicles sub-market, maintain a strong position in the attractive forest-vehicle sub-market

Figure 9.7: The effects of the five options on market position

	Profit im-provement	Investment	Disinvest-ment	Redundan-cies	Market posi-tions	Know-how
1a Radical disin-vestment	7.35 million	—	25 million	145	1 market; maintenance of niche po-sitions	Loss of chassis know-how
1b Radical disin-vestment and dou-ble-shift produc-tion	9.35 million	—	25 million	110	1 market; enlargement of niche positions	Loss of chassis Know-how
2 Abandon unprofit-able products	7.5 million	4 million	—	50	2 markets; enlargement of niche positions	Preserve chassis know-how
3a Abandon unprofit-able products and sell the Zu-rich plant	5.2 million	5 million	22 million	95	2 markets; enlargement of niche positions	Preserve chassis know-how
3b Abandon unprofit-able prod-ucts, sell the Zurich plant + in-troduce double-shift pro-duction	7.4 million	5 million	22 million	50	2 markets; enlargement of niche po-sitions	Preserve chassis know-how

Figure 9.8: The completed consequence matrix

- Of the remaining two options, 1b and 3b, the former is financially more attractive in the short term. It allows higher disinvestments, requires no new investments and eliminates sources of loss. However, option 3b creates the possibility of re-launching the company in chassis construction through a strategy of concentration. If this succeeds, the company would stand on three legs instead of just two. What is more, 60 jobs would be saved. Should the attempt fail, they would have to move to option 1b quickly. In this case, the costs of moving production from Zurich, 5 million Swiss francs, would also have to be written off.

Dr. Herren asks Mr. Walther to produce a report within a week. This will be introduced at the next board meeting and also used in meetings with the banks and trade unions. The report should include:

- the company's financial statement, supplemented by the contribution margin figures for the four chassis types
- a presentation of the five options
- the evaluation of the options
- the proposed decision, with reasons.

Part Three: Special issues and approaches to resolving them

Two important issues were excluded from Part One and Part Two in order to keep the text clear. First, when working on a decision, the question often arises as to whether the problem should be resolved on the basis of existing information or whether new information should be obtained before making the decision. This is a problem at the "meta" level which is extremely important in practice, and which remains for us to deal with. A second critical area which was not dealt with in the earlier chapters is that of group or collective decision-making: many vital decisions are made by groups.

In Part Three we examine these two important issues. After reading Part Three the reader:

- will understand the nature of information procurement decisions, and how they should be approached
- will have an overview of the problems in group decision-making and be familiar with procedures and rules for group-based decisions.

Part III has two chapters:

- Chapter 10 deals with information procurement. It begins by identifying information procurement as a decision at the meta-level in problem-solving processes. Next, practical help is offered on how to approach information procurement decisions. The recommendations are based to some extent on the practical experience of the authors, but also draw on work by Bayes. This approach, which is based on a number of restrictive conditions, is presented separately as an inset in the main text.
- Chapter 11 is concerned with collective decisions. First we define collective decisions and show their importance. Next we consider goal systems within groups and group decision behaviour. Finally, a longer section presents approaches to determining collective decisions. In this section we first summarise work by Arrow, who has formulated a number of requirements for sensible and democratic collective decisions but also demonstrated that these conditions can

never all be met. We then conclude by presenting both a number of classical rules and several more complex approaches.

10 Information procurement decisions

10.1 Information procurement as a decision at the meta-level

When tackling a decision problem, the actor always has to work on two levels:

- The first is the problem itself: the actor has to analyse and understand the problem, to identify solution options, to assess these and finally to make a decision.
- In addition there will be a number of tasks at the meta-level. We have already seen that the problem-solving work must be planned; the various tasks will need to be allocated to different staff and this work must be coordinated. A further major task at the meta-level is to decide whether to proceed with problem-solving on the basis of existing information or whether the level of information should first be improved.

New information may come from internal or external sources and may vary in its degree of detail and in its reliability. In problem analysis, and when developing options, there are choices to be made about how detailed the information base must be. However, the pivotal meta-decision for procurement or non-procurement of additional information is required at the stage of the evaluation of options. The question is this: Should the final decision be based on the already-known consequences or should one invest additional resources in getting more detailed information about the effects of the options?

The more that is invested in information procurement, the greater the probability that good options will be found and the best one selected. However, the procurement of additional information inevitably involves additional expense. Moreover it prolongs the procedure for resolving the problem and thereby delays a decision. How great these disadvantages are will depend very much on the type of problem.

To decide whether to obtain additional information is simple in principle. Obtaining new information always makes sense if the additional benefits it brings outweigh the costs involved. If this is not the case, one should desist. But a general statement of this kind needs to be extended by more detailed recommendations of how this rule may be applied in particular cases.

10.2   Recommendations for decisions on information procurement

The best-known principles for making information procurement decisions were developed by Bayes and these principles are introduced in **Inset 10.1**. Since Bayes' ideas are subject to a large number of conditions, some of which are highly restrictive, they are rarely directly applicable. What we have done here is to draw out some generalizations from Bayes and combine these with our own experience to produce a set of recommendations for making information procurement decisions.

Inset 10.1: Bayes's approach for establishing the value of additional information

In order to be able to make specific recommendations, Bayes formulates a number of assumptions, some of which are highly restrictive:

1. First we must note that all Bayes's principles are valid only for univalent risk decisions (Weibel, 1978, p. 11). In other words Bayes assumes that the actor only has to deal with a single decision criterion and will be required to evaluate the options for a number of scenarios for which probability values are available.

2. Bayes assumes, moreover, that the actor already knows the options, the environmental scenarios and their probabilities, and the consequence values and would therefore be able to make the decision on the basis of this information. The question at issue is whether he/she should judge on the basis of the present decision matrix, or whether it is worthwhile postponing the decision and improving the quality of the decision matrix through the procurement of additional information. With this exclusive focus on the decision matrix, Bayes ignores the question of additional information in earlier phases of the decision-making procedure: the steps of analysing the problem and of developing options.

3. Bayes's consideration of the question of procurement of additional information addresses only the probabilities for the different scenarios. In contrast, the additional investment in information does not produce any improvement in the consequence values (von Nitzsch, 2002, p. 220 ff.).

4. The fourth premise concerns the decision maxim applied by the actor. Bayes assumes that the actor uses the expectation value maxim to calculate the overall consequences of the options (Weibel, 1978, p. 20). However, as shown in Chapter 8, the use of this maxim can be problematic.

5. Another assumption is that a problem has only two options "do something/do nothing" (Weibel, 1978, p. 21).

6. Finally, Bayes opts not to include the dimension of time in his considerations. He thereby effectively excludes the important question of the effect of postponing the decision.

The approach used by Bayes to resolve the information procurement question consists of calculating the expectation value with information procurement and comparing it with the expectation value of the best option without information procurement. How the expectation value with information procurement is to be calculated is shown on the basis of an example from von Nitzsch (2002, p. 220 ff.). In the presentation below we have avoided the special terminology introduced by Bayes and adopted by von Nitzsch. We have also tried to keep the number of symbols to a minimum.

In this example a company is faced with a decision about whether to launch a new product. **Figure 10.1** shows the actor's decision matrix.

If we use the maxim of expectation value, then the product should clearly be launched. The expectation value amounts to €100 million against an expectation value of zero if the company decides not to introduce the product.

However, since launching the product may incur a loss of 50 million with a probability of 0.4, the actor takes on a significant risk in

Criteria, scenarios and probabilities	Profit in millions of euro	
	Launch successful	Launch unsuccessful
Options	0.6	0.4
Launch product	+ 200	- 50
Don't launch product	0	0

Figure 10.1: Decision matrix for a product launch problem

going for that option. This may induce him to obtain additional information, thereby reducing the risk in the decision. Here, the actor has the possibility of commissioning a market research study at a cost of €2 million. This study will either recommend introducing the product or will advise against it. The actor also has information regarding the accuracy of such a study (von Nitzsch, 2002, p. 220):

- Advice in favour of the launch will be correct in 90% of cases, thus correctly anticipating a successful product launch. However, this means that for 10% of successful launches, the study will advise against.
- An unsuccessful product launch can be predicted with an even greater probability of 95%. This means that for 5% of launches that turn out to be unsuccessful the study will recommend in favour of the product launch.

The actor in this case now has three courses of action:

1. Decide to launch the product.
2. Decide not to launch the product.
3. Postpone the decision and commission the study.

If the third course of action is chosen, the choice between 1 and 2 will be made after the study has been completed on the basis of a better level of information about these options.

If a study is commissioned, the actor will be confronted with a series of decisions. Such problems can no longer be represented in the form of a decision matrix but must be represented visually as a decision tree. **Figure 10.2** presents the decision tree for this decision problem, which includes the alternative of commissioning a study. The illustration gives an overview of the problem structure and presents both existing information and information still missing. The expectation value of the third option, which is required for the decision, is missing, as are a number of probability values. The expectation value of the third option, the study, can only be calculated if the probabilities which are still missing can be determined.

The probabilities that the market study will recommend for or against the introduction of the product can now be determined as follows:

- The actor knows that the probability that the product launch will be successful is 0.6 and the probability that it will be unsuccessful is 0.4.
- Furthermore, the actor knows that the study can predict a successful launch with a probability of 0.9 and an unsuccessful one with a probability of 0.95.
- These two pieces of information are now brought together in **Figure 10.3**. The illustration shows that the probability that the study will recommend in favour of the introduction of the product is 0.56 and the probability that it will advise against it is 0.44.

To find the expectation value of the study, four more probabilities now have to be calculated:

- Probability of a successful outcome on the basis of a study advising the introduction of the product.
- Probability of an unsuccessful outcome on the basis of a study advising the introduction of the product.
- Probability of a successful outcome on the basis of a study advising against the introduction of the product.
- Probability of an unsuccessful outcome on the basis of a study advising against the introduction of the product.

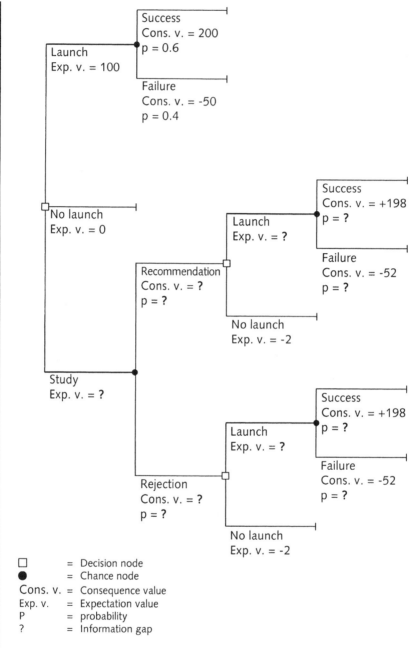

Figure 10.2: Decision tree with information gaps
(adapted from von Nitzsch, 2002, p. 221)

	Launch successful 0.6	Launch unsuccessful 0.4	Total
Study advises launch	correctly 0.9	incorrectly 0.05	—
	0.6 x 0.9 = 0.54	0.4 x 0.05 = 0.02	0.56
Study advises against launch	incorrectly 0.1	correctly 0.95	—
	0.6 x 0.1 = 0.06	0.4 x 0.95 = 0.38	0.44
Total	1	1	—
	—	—	1

All figures are probabilities

Figure 10.3: Calculation of the probabilities for studies advising in favour and against product launches
(adapted from von Nitzsch, 2002, p. 222)

Figure **10.4** summarizes the results of the calculation of these four probability values. In the figure, the studies whose findings are correct and those which turn out to be misleading are each broken down as advising in favour or against the launch (von Nitzsch, 2002, p. 222).

The decision tree can now be worked through from right to left on the basis of these six probability values. As **Figure 10.5** shows, should the study recommend going ahead with the product, the

	Launch successful 0.6	Launch unsuccessful 0.4	Total
Study advises product launch	0.54	0.02	0.56
	0.54 / 0.56 = 0.964	0.02 / 0.56 = 0.036	1
Study advises against product launch	0.06	0.38	0.44
	0.06 / 0.44 = 0.136	0.38 / 0.44 = 0.864	1
Total	—	—	—
	—	—	1

All figures are probabilities

Figure 10.4: Calculation of the probabilities of successful and unsuccessful product launches based on positive and negative studies (adapted from von Nitzsch, 2002, p. 222).

expectation value would be €189 million as against an expectation value of €-2 million if the market launch were abandoned. The actor would therefore launch the product. If, however the study advises against launching the product, the expectation value is €-18 million if the product launch nevertheless goes ahead. This expected loss contrasts with an expectation value of €-2 million if the product launch is abandoned. Thus the actor will abandon the launch if the study advises against.

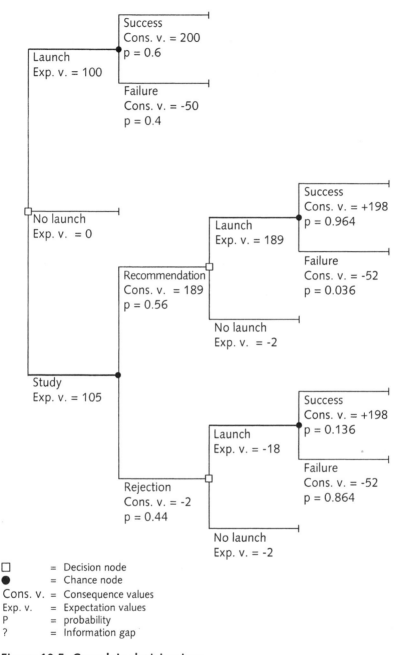

Figure 10.5: Complete decision tree
(adapted from von Nitzsch, 2002, p. 223)

The expectation value for the study itself can now be calculated; this calculation assumes that the actor will go ahead with the product launch if the study's recommendation is positive and forego the launch if the recommendation is negative:

€ 189 million • 0.56 + (€ -2 million) • 0.44 = € 105 million

This calculation shows that it is worthwhile for the actor to invest €2 million in the study and to make the decision on the launch of the product on the basis of the study's recommendation (von Nitzsch, 2002, p. 223).

In summary, it can be said that Bayes has developed a method for determining the expectation value of information procurement measures. The approach is based on the assumption that the actor can determine the reliability of the information which can be procured (von Nitzsch, 2002, p. 227 ff.).

If an actor is confronted with the question of the procurement of additional information in the course of the treatment of a decision problem, it is advisable to work through the following four steps, presented in **Figure 10.6** (Kühn & Fankhauser, 1996, p. 137 ff.).

Considerations for costs and benefits of the procurement of additional information will only be worthwhile if the actor can specify a procedure for the information procurement and if the time frame allows such measures. For this reason it is worth first making a rough assessment of the feasibility of the information procurement.

- To this purpose, the information required must first be specified. In the problem analysis step, for example, a need may arise for quantitative information concerning market volumes and market shares. Or when determining the consequences of different options, the effects of price changes on demand will need to be predicted.
- After this rough specification of information needs, the actor must discover whether or not there is at least one way of proceeding to obtain the relevant information. It is also necessary to specify the time that this will require. The time spent on information procurement is especially important when outside circumstances mean that

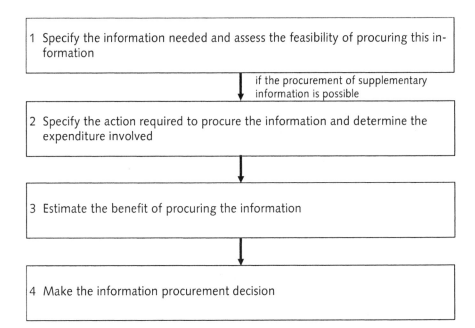

1 Specify the information needed and assess the feasibility of procuring this information

if the procurement of supplementary information is possible

2 Specify the action required to procure the information and determine the expenditure involved

3 Estimate the benefit of procuring the information

4 Make the information procurement decision

Figure 10.6: Procedure for making a decision about information procurement

a decision is required within a certain period. This is the case, for example, with decisions about acquisitions, when offers are only valid for a short period. Time is also important when a threat problem seems to be escalating and must therefore be solved quickly; this could be a quality defect in a mass consumer item that is already on sale. To summarise, information procurement is not always feasible, either because no procedure exists or because the timeframe for the decision will not allow it.

Where measures for the procurement of additional information appear feasible, the second step is to determine the methods to be employed and their costs. In some circumstances, the information to be obtained must first be specified more closely. This is because the specific types of data required may determine the selection of the method of data procurement and in turn affect the costs involved. To take an example, a detailed account of market structure can be obtained by quantifying product groups (sub-markets) and/or client groups (customer segments). Often secondary data will be available for the determination of the sub-markets, which means that extensive research is not required. In contrast, precise reliable data on client groups typically requires field research with a large sample. This incurs significantly higher costs and of course also involves a time delay. Often information procurement will be carried out by market research companies. The costs of this can normally be determined by inviting bids. There are, however, many information needs that are better fulfilled by internal staff. Here it must be decided who can carry out each of the different information procurement tasks and what the internal costs will be.

In Step 3 the actor has to evaluate the benefits of information procurement. This essentially depends on two things:

- The significance of the consequences of a wrong decision: a strategic decision with millions at stake will justify greater investment in information procurement than a decision with consequences in the region of a few thousand euro.
- The possible improvement of the quality of the decision as a result of the information obtained: when assessing this, it is important to take into account the stage in the decision-making procedure for which the information is required.

It is usually possible to determine the approximate order of magnitude of the effects of a wrong decision. One can get a good idea of this by asking whether the difference between a good and a bad problem solution lies in tens of thousands or hundreds of thousands of euro. Although it is difficult to assess how far the procurement of information will improve the quality of the decision, the actor should be able to make a rough estimate of whether the additional information will allow a significant improvement of his/her understanding of the problem and of how to quantify the consequences of the options. A significant improvement is required, otherwise it is not worth considering the procurement of new information.

To make the decision in Step 4, the actor has to weigh the costs and benefits of information procurement. Since the benefits of the information can usually only be determined in terms of an approximate order of magnitude which essentially depends on the magnitude of the consequences of a wrong decision, information procurement measures are normally judged summarily. The magnitude of the consequences of a wrong decision is compared with the costs of the information procurement, which can usually be estimated quite accurately. In general, one will decide in favour of procuring information if the consequences of a wrong decision clearly surpass the costs of information procurement.

11 Collective decisions

11.1 Collective decisions and their growing importance in companies

In business it is becoming increasingly common for problems to be solved by a group of people. However, under the heading of collective decisions we may find a variety of very different phenomena. Following Brauchlin (1990, p. 250 ff.) and von Nitzsch (2002, p. 61), collective decisions can be classified according to three dimensions, and these are presented in **Figure 11.1**. The illustration shows in bold type the three characteristics of the type of collective decision which we focus on in this chapter:

- In business, a decision is considered a collective decision if it involves a group of between three and around twenty.
- The groups are formally established committees or working groups to which tasks are assigned and whose areas of authority and responsibility are well defined. The range of such groups is very wide, including boards, top management teams, divisional management teams, project steering groups and special committees.
- It is axiomatic that the goal systems of the group members should be aligned as regards the essential points. However, it would not be realistic to imagine that all group members have an identical view of the targets. We must recognise differences, both in individual goals and in the interpretation of goals. The idea of the goal system of a decision group is taken up again in subsection 11.2.1 below.

In recent decades a greater tendency towards collective decisions has been observed in the business world. A number of different factors have brought about this change:

- The tendency to concentration in business means that there are fewer and fewer businesses which are owned by an individual or in which one individual has the final say. If there are a number of important groupings among the owners, these will usually all be represented on the board and be involved in important decisions. In the case of a public company, the board normally represents not only the owners but also all important stakeholder groups.

Parameters	Values			
Number of people involved	Dyad; 2 people	**Group; 3 to approx. 20 people**		Organised systems; from approx. 20 up to millions of people
Type of group	**Formal group**		Informal group	
Goals	Fully congruent	**Congruent in essential points**	Divergent in some essential points	Totally divergent

Bold = the three characteristics of the type of collective decision discussed in this chapter

Figure 11.1: Parameters of collective decisions and associated values
(adapted from Brauchlin, 1990, p. 250 ff. and von Nitzsch, 2002, p. 61)

- There is a general increasing desire to offer a number of people the opportunity to take part in the decision process (Brauchlin, 1990, p. 154). This is an expression of the political ideals of democracy.
- More and more individual employees want to be involved in company decisions. This is first of all a question of the personal prestige of the individual. But participation in the decision process also offers employees the opportunity to advance their own interests (Brauchlin, 1990, p. 254).
- The increasing popularity of collective decision-making in business is frequently justified by arguing that it leads to better decisions. Whether this is true is debatable. Committee-based decision-making has a number of serious disadvantages in comparison to individual decision-making. The advantages and disadvantages of the two types of decisions are discussed in subsection 11.2.2.

11.2   Group goal systems and group decision behaviour

11.2.1 Group goal systems

Even when the actor is an individual, his or her view of the target situation will not be precise and may contain contradictions. When the actor is a collective the situation is even more difficult, as differences of opinion will be found to exist between the group members. **Figure 11.2** shows the goal system of an actor which consists of three individuals. We note that:

- Not all members of the group need to pursue all goals. For example, above-average wages and social benefits is a target only for A, while above-average return on capital is an objective only for B and C.
- The actors' views of the concrete content of a goal are also never completely congruent. Here, all three are united in considering high quality an important goal. For one of them, this means not just careful production and tight quality control, but also requires using only the very best materials. However, for the second group member, high quality can be achieved with standard materials as long as they are carefully processed and the products are thoroughly checked. For the third group member quality refers not just to the products themselves, but also includes customer advice and full after-sales service.
- There may be contradictions between the goals of the different members of the collective. The goal of above-average wages and social benefits pursued by A is at least partly in conflict with B and C's goal of achieving an above-average return on capital.
- Conflicting objectives held by the same individual will also occur in the collective goal system. A, B and C all pursue the goals "Concentration in Western Europe" and "Growth well above average", but these two goals may be contradictory.
- Finally, the goal system will include differences between individuals as regards how precise their views are of the content of the various goals.

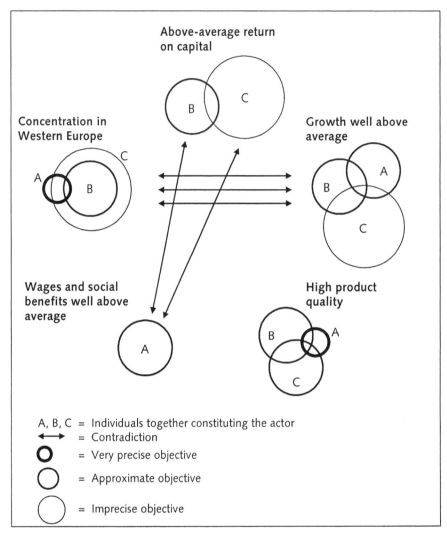

Figure 11.2: Goal system for an actor composed of several people

11.2.2 Group decision behaviour

When groups are entrusted with decisions, the decision behaviour is different to what is seen with individuals. Group decisions are a complex many-layered phenomenon and empirical research only ever examines individual questions, so it is difficult to give an overview of the effects of collective decision making. **Figure 11.3** is an attempt to give an overview. The authors are conscious, that the figure remains incomplete and the different cause-effect relationships depicted here remain somewhat controversial.

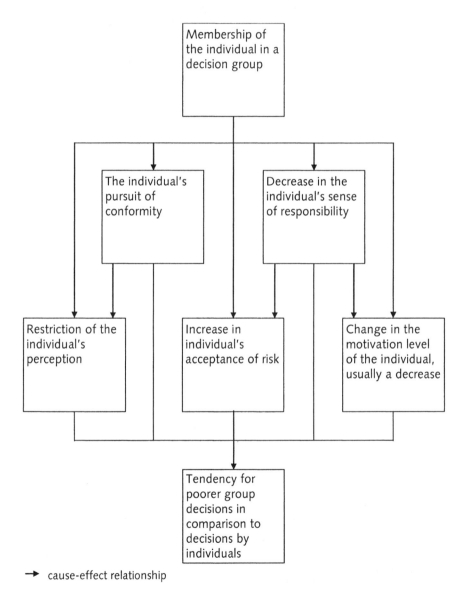

→ cause-effect relationship

Figure 11.3: Tendency towards poorer decisions by a group compared to an individual

It is known from research that members of a group strive for conformity. To this end, group members are ready to shift their values and objectives. If harmony in the group appears extremely important to a group member, he or she may even, more or less consciously, ignore or misrepresent facts. **Inset 11.1** presents an experiment carried out by Asch, which confirms this surprising finding, that not just values and goals but even facts may be sacrificed for group conformity (von Nitzsch, 2002, p. 63).

Inset 11.1: Asch's experiment on group members' pursuit of conformity
(Text based on von Nitzsch, 2002 p. 63 f.)

In Asch's experiment (1955), subjects had to compare the length of a line with the length of three option lines A, B and C, and declare which of the three it matched. Since these three option lines differed conspicuously in length, the task was easy to solve and yielded an error-rate of just 0.7% in individual tests.

Afterwards, the subjects were put into groups of seven people. The subject occupied the sixth position, while the other six members of the group were accomplices of the investigators. The estimates of these accomplices were communicated openly. After twelve rounds during which the accomplices always gave the right answer, six further rounds followed in which they all named the same wrong line. Although in principle the task was just as easy to solve in a group as individually, the rate of incorrect answers for the subjects climbed to 37%, and 75% of the subjects made a mistake at least once.

The pursuit of conformity usually only involves verbal statements and external behaviour, but does not include the underlying values and reflections. In this case, one speaks of compliance. It is however possible in the longer term that the group modifies values and thinking and brings about acceptance of the group norms by its individual members (von Nitzsch, 2002, p. 63 ff.).

Membership of the group leads not only to the desire for homogeneity but also brings about changes in the individual group member's sense of responsibility. The individual can hide behind the group, as the group situation leads to diffuse responsibilities in the sense that the individual group member does not feel solely responsible but merely jointly responsible (Brauchlin, 1990, p. 261).

A third effect of being in a group involves restrictions on the group members' perceptions of the reality of the decision situation. This phenomenon can be fatal for effective decision-making. It has three basic causes (von Nitzsch, 2002, p. 75 ff):

- The need for conformity can lead to the group neglecting to deal with uncomfortable facts. The decision-makers are consequently less well informed than they could be. The fact that negative elements may be missing from the picture is especially worrying, as these would often influence the decision.
- The pursuit of conformity also means that agreeing votes prevail in group discussions. This gives the group members too much self-confidence; the individual assumes that so many people cannot be mistaken (von Nitzsch, 2002, p. 75).
- Finally group members are inclined to value statements from people within the group more than those from people outside the group. This in-group bias automatically prevents the group from taking on board any dissenting views which do not conform to those of the group" (von Nitzsch, 2002, p. 75).

A fourth consequence of group decisions is a higher readiness to accept risk. This risk-shift effect is partly the result of group responsibility as opposed to individual responsibility. In addition, people with a higher inclination for risk normally have greater weight within the group than group members who are risk-shy (Brauchlin, 1990, p. 261; von Nitzsch, 2002, p. 75).

Finally, the group influences the motivation of the group members (von Nitzsch, 2002, p. 67 ff.).

- High group cohesion can work to encourage and increase the motivation of the individuals.

- The opposite is more frequent however: unconsciously or consciously, motivation is reduced by membership in the group. Collective responsibility means that group members unconsciously reduce their involvement. This phenomenon has been termed 'social loafing'. However, individual group members can also consciously behave as mere passengers, allowing the others to take on the work. In the long term such behaviour, termed free-riding, may reduce the motivation of the other group members. They may even consciously decide to reduce their own efforts in order not to feel exploited. This has been termed the sucker effect.

The collapse of Swissair, the former Swiss national carrier, provides an interesting example of group decision behaviour. Subsequent analysis showed that the decision behaviour of Swissair's board played an essential role in the downfall of the company:

- Asking awkward questions or expressing divergent opinions was evidently frowned upon and therefore happened only rarely.
- A number of board members failed to attend meetings, or left early when important decisions were made, such as the purchase of LTU. This shows that individual board members did not feel full personal responsibility for decisions.
- The investigating authorities found that on a number of occasions decisions were made to acquire companies without sufficient information being available about the accompanying liabilities. Furthermore, the board was also not adequately informed about the effective return flow from the acquisitions in comparison to the estimates used for planning.
- In retrospect, it is obvious that the hunter strategy pursued by Swissair was a high risk strategy. It seems possible that the comparatively high risk-acceptance of the Swissair board could be attributed to the risk-shift effect typical of collective decision-making.
- The motivation and the involvement of the board members are difficult to judge in retrospect. But it is assumed that these varied greatly.

This leaves the difficult question of what can be done to limit as far as possible the negative effects of group decision behaviour. We see two possible approaches:

- All the facts must be on the table; a group culture must be developed which allows divergent views. This can be promoted by applying rules. For example, there could be a rule that group members give their views on certain questions before a meeting.
- It is a good idea to try to strengthen the sense of responsibility of the individual group members. This can be promoted by using the minutes to record individuals' comments and votes. Another possibility is that the group should delegate certain decision problems to subgroups or to individual group members.

11.3   Rules for making collective decisions

11.3.1 Differing individual orders of preference as starting point

The rules we will now present for making collective decisions only concern the final step in the decision process, in which the best option is chosen. They are only applicable if the group did not reach a consensus in the earlier phases of the decision process. In fact, the group members' pursuit of conformity normally means that the group will agree on an option in the course of the treatment of the decision problem and a final vote is typically no longer necessary.

In a minority of cases, however, the group-members will have different preferences. These differences imply the need for rules for arriving at a collective decision. We are concerning ourselves here with a problem which is not very frequent, but which, when it does occur, is likely to be very significant. It is not only important that the group should arrive at a clear and sound decision regarding the problem. The way in which the decision is made will also be important for the future working climate within the group.

Each group member will have an order of preference which indicates how the options would be ranked if the person was judging alone. If the group has two options a and b, any given group member may:
- prefer a to b
- prefer b to a
- consider a and b equivalent

With just two options, a group-member has to choose between three possible orders of preference or rankings. But if three different options are open to the group, there are 13 possible orders of preference for each member to consider (Bamberg & Coenenberg, 2002, p. 25 ff.; Rommelfanger & Eickemeier, 2002, p. 192 ff.)

Furthermore, if the decision committee consists of three members (X, Y and Z), and there are two options (a and b), then this means that 27 different configurations or preference-profiles are possible, for example:
- X, Y and Z can prefer a to b
- X and Y can prefer a to b, while Z prefers b to a

and so on.

With three decision options, a, b, and c, and three group members, the number of possible configurations climbs to 13^3, which is 2,197 (Bamberg & Coenenberg, 2002, p. 252; Rommelfanger & Eickemeier, 2002, p. 193 ff.).

In this situation the starting point for any collective decision will be the individual orders of preference of the group members. All of these together give the configuration or preference-profile for the group. To reach a collective decision we have to produce the collective order of preference or we have at least to determine the best option from the group point of view. A rule-based procedure is required in either case. However, before looking at possible rules, we should first consider what requirements such rules must seek to satisfy.

11.3.2 Requirements for forming a collective order of preference

Arrow (1963) defined four conditions for sensible democratic rules for deriving a collective order of preference from individual rankings (Bamberg & Coenenberg, 2002, p. 255 ff.; Rommelfanger & Eicke-meier, 2002, p. 198 ff.):

1. The rule system should be able to produce a "collective order of preference" or "collective ranking" for every possible configuration of "individual orders of preference" or "individual rankings". As we

saw, with a three-member group evaluating three options, there are as many as 2,197 different possible configurations. This first requirement means that the rule system must be able to produce a collective ranking for any of these configurations.

2. The second requirement is that if each individual ranks a above b, then the collective ranking must also rank a above b.

3. Arrows' third stipulation is that where two different configurations match in the preference order of two options a and b, the two collective orders of preference must also match in the preference order of a and b. This means preferences other than a and b, for which the two configurations may differ, will not influence the ranking of a and b in the two collective orders of preference. **Inset 11.2** presents an example of this rather complicated requirement, known as the "independence of irrelevant options".

4. The fourth and final requirement is that no one group member can have special status. If, for example, each preference of member X automatically becomes a component of the collective order of preference, X would have a dictatorial position. Under these conditions, the preferences of the other group members would only play a role in relation to the options to which X would be indifferent.

Inset 11.2: The independence of irrelevant options as a requirement for forming a collective order of preference
(Text based on Bamberg & Coenenberg, 2002, p. 256 ff.)

The requirement of the independence of irrelevant options means that if two configurations agree in the preference order of two options, the collective orders of preference established for each of the two groups must also agree in the preference order of the two options. Differing preferences within the two profiles in reference to other options may not change this.

Figure 11.4 shows two configurations, each of which represents three group members faced with three options a, b and c. As the illustration shows, the two configurations are in agreement as far as a and b are concerned: in each configuration, two group members prefer a to b, while the third group member prefers b to a.

	Configuration A			Configuration B		
	X	Y	Z	U	V	W
1. Preference	a	a	c	c	c	b
2. Preference	b	b	b	a	a	a
3. Preference	c	c	a	b	b	c
X, Y and Z = members of the first decision group U, V and W = members of a second decision group a, b and c = options						

Figure 11.4: Configurations of two groups of three people ranking three options
(adapted from Bamberg & Coenenberg, 2002, p. 156)

Arrow's requirement is that in each of these two cases the rule system should produce a collective order of preference in which the relative positions of a and b are the same. Since two of the three group members prefer a to b, the two collective orders of preference may prefer a to b. But as the three group members are not united in reference to a and b, it is also possible that the two collective orders of preference will show no preference between a and b.

The independence of irrelevant options simply means that Arrow has ruled out the possibility that for instance in one collective order of preference a will be preferred to b while in the other the two options a and b are viewed as equivalent.

If a procedure for aggregating the individual rankings of a decision-making group is to be sensible and democratic, it seems plausible to require that all four of these requirements should be met. However, supported by contributions from other researchers, Arrow (1963) has succeeded in proving that an aggregation procedure that meets all four requirements only exists for the special case of two options. The aggregation mechanism for this special case is very simple moreover; it is a majority decision. As soon as three or more options are included in the selection, no aggregation mechanism is able to meet all four requirements at the same time (Bamberg & Coenenberg, 2002, p. 257 ff.).

11.3.3 Classic rules for the formation of a collective order of preference or for determining the option preferred by the collective

As we have seen, there is no aggregation mechanism that simultaneously fulfils all of Arrow's four requirements for sensible and democratic collective decisions. Nevertheless, as there are many groups in organizations which have to make collective decisions, we will now present rule systems which will help to make group decisions possible, even though they do not meet all Arrow's requirements. These rule systems can be classified according to whether they:

- produce a collective order of preference for the options
- or simply determine the group's preferred option.

A simple method is the simple majority: each group member votes and the option that gets the most votes is chosen. If two options share first position, the chairperson decides. Alternatively, there is a second vote which considers only these two options. If there is again a tie, the chairperson has the casting vote.

The simple majority method is easily understood and leads to a decision. Its disadvantage is that it only yields the one preferred option and says nothing about the order of preference of the remaining options. If the chosen option later proves impossible to implement, then another vote must be taken.

It is possible to insist on an absolute majority or even unanimity. The disadvantage of this is that often no decision can be made and the matter has to be adjourned. For this reason it is unusual in company decisions to demand either an absolute majority of the votes or unanimity. In order to prevent chance decisions, however, a quorum can be required.

Borda presents an alternative approach. His proposal is that each member of the group should allocate points to each option: the worst option receives one point, the second worst two points, and so on. With five options, the preferred option will get five points. The collective order of preference can now be determined by adding the points for each option and sorting the options according to their scores (Bamberg & Coenenberg, 2002, p. 263 ff.; Rommelfanger & Eicke-meier, 2002, p. 195 ff.). This is a simple procedure which not only determines the preferred option but also yields an order of preference. This makes it somewhat surprising that it is not used in business more often.

Another method, and one frequently used in practice, requires the use of pairs of options for comparison. It begins with the comparison of two options. The winning option is then compared to a third option and so on. The option that wins in the final comparison is chosen (Bamberg & Coenenberg, 2002, p. 265 ff.; Rommelfanger & Eicke-meier, 2002, p. 196).

If there is one option that a majority of the decision group considers better than all the others, then this will always win with pair compari-son. If no such absolutely superior option exists, however, the result may depend on chance or be subject to influence from the chairper-son. Condorcet discovered this over 200 years ago. **Inset 11.3** de-scribes his "voting paradox".

Inset 11.3: Condorcet's voting paradox
(Text based on Bamberg & Coenenberg, 2002, p. 253 ff.)

Figure 11.5 shows the configuration of three people in reference to three options. As can be seen from the illustration:
- X and Z prefer option a to option b,
- X and Y prefer option b to option c and
- Y and Z prefer option c to option a.

If the first vote takes place between a and b, a wins. This option will then be matched against c, and c will be chosen. However, if one first matches b and c, b is preferred. Then, subsequently, when

	X	Y	Z
1. Preference	a	b	c
2. Preference	b	c	a
3. Preference	c	a	b
X, Y and Z = members of the decision group a, b and c = options			

Figure 11.5: The configuration underlying Condorcet's voting paradox

b is compared to a, a will be chosen. If the chairperson would like to see option b win, he or she may first require a pair comparison between a and c. As a result of this way of proceeding, b will win because it is superior to c.

The conclusion from Condorcet's paradox is simple: If no absolutely superior option exists, the option which is chosen will be a matter of chance or within the power of the chairperson. It is possible to draw lots to determine the options for the initial pair comparison, but all that this means is that in this case the winning option is a chance result. The chairperson can determine the sequence that will allow his preferred option to win provided he knows the preferences of the group members and sets up the vote sequence accordingly.

11.3.4 More complex procedures for the formation of the collective order of preference

We end this chapter with two more complex approaches to the formation of a collective order of preference. One is based on the preference relations described by Blin & Whinston (1974) and the other is Saaty's (1980) analytical hierarchical process.

Blin & Whinston (1974) propose using the individual orders of preference to determine patterns of preference with the group. These patterns are afterwards the basis for determining the collective order of preference. **Inset 11.4** presents an example of this approach, which is based on Fuzzy Logic.

Inset 11.4: Blin and Whinston's preference patterns
(Text based on Rommelfanger & Eickemeier, 2002, p. 207 ff.)

A group of ten people have to rank four truck models. **Figure 11.6** shows the individual orders of preference of the ten persons.

	Q	R	S	T	U	V	W	X	Y	Z
1. Preference	a	d	d	d	a	c	d	d	a	d
2. Preference	b	c	c	c	b	a	a	a	d	a
3. Preference	d	a	a	a	d	b	c	c	c	b
4. Preference	c	b	b	b	c	d	b	b	b	c

X, Y ... Z   = members of the decision group
a, b, c and d = options

Figure 11.6: Individual orders of preference
(adapted from Rommelfanger & Eickemeier, 2002, p. 210)

As can be seen from the illustration, all ten group members prefer a to b, while only six prefer a to c. By analyzing the rankings in this way, a matrix with the preference patterns of the group can be produced. This is shown in **Figure 11.7**.

In the next step, all the collective orders of preference are now determined that are compatible with the highest intensity of preference. The highest intensity of preference favours a over b by 10:0. Twelve collective orders of preference are compatible with this:
(a > b > c > d), (a > b > d > c), (a > c > b > d)
(a > c > d > b), (a > d > b > c), (a > d > c > b)
(c > a > b > d), (c > a > d > b), (c > d > a > b)
(d > a > b > c), (d > a > c > b), (d > c > a > b)

Preferred to	a	b	c	d
a	–	10 : 0	6 : 4	4 : 6
b	0 : 10	–	3 : 7	3 : 7
c	4 : 6	7 : 3	–	1 : 9
d	6 : 4	7 : 3	9 : 1	–
a, b, c and d = options				

Figure 11.7: The preference patterns of the group

In the next step, from these twelve collective orders of preference are selected all those orders that are also compatible with the second-highest preference intensity. This is the preference for d over c by 9:1. Based on this, six of the twelve orders of preference must be ruled out. The following six collective orders of preference remain in the race:

(a > b > d > c), (a > d > b > c), (a > d > c > b)
(d > a > b > c), (d > a > c > b), (d > c > a > b)

The third highest preference intensity is 7:3 for c over b and also for d over b. Taking both of these into account simultaneously, only three collective orders of preference remain:

(a > d > c > b), (d > a > c > b), (d > c > a > b)

The fourth highest intensity is also shared by two preferences: a is preferred to c, as is d to a, with an intensity of 6:4. Only the collective order of preference:

(d > a > c > b)

simultaneously accommodates these two preference intensities. It thus becomes the collective order of preference.

Figure 11.8 shows that Blin and Whinston's procedure is sensible. In the illustration the sum of the preference intensities underlying all 24 possible orders of preference is determined. The chosen order of preference has the highest preference-intensity.

Order of preference	Preference intensities underlying the order of preference	Sum of the preference intensities
a>b>c>d	1.0 + 0.6 + 0.4 + 0.3 + 0.3 + 0.1	2.7
a>b>d>c	1.0 + 0.4 + 0.6 + 0.3 + 0.3 + 0.9	3.5
a>c>b>d	0.6 + 1.0 + 0.4 + 0.7 + 0.1 + 0.3	3.1
a>c>d>b	0.6 + 0.4 + 1.0 + 0.1 + 0.7 + 0.7	3.5
a>d>b>c	0.4 + 1.0 + 0.6 + 0.7 + 0.9 + 0.3	3.9
a>d>c>b	0.4 + 0.6 + 1.0 + 0.9 + 0.7 + 0.7	4.3
b>a>c>d	0.0 + 0.3 + 0.3 + 0.6 + 0.4 + 0.1	1.7
b>a>d>c	0.0 + 0.3 + 0.3 + 0.4 + 0.6 + 0.9	2.5
b>c>a>d	0.3 + 0.0 + 0.3 + 0.4 + 0.1 + 0.4	1.5
b>c>d>a	0.3 + 0.3 + 0.0 + 0.1 + 0.4 + 0.6	1.7
b>d>a>c	0.3 + 0.0 + 0.3 + 0.6 + 0.9 + 0.6	2.7
b>d>c>a	0.3 + 0.3 + 0.0 + 0.9 + 0.6 + 0.4	2.5
c>a>b>d	0.4 + 0.7 + 0.1 + 1.0 + 0.4 + 0.3	2.9
c>a>d>b	0.4 + 0.1 + 0.7 + 0.4 + 1.0 + 0.7	3.3
c>b>a>d	0.7 + 0.4 + 0.1 + 0.0 + 0.3 + 0.4	1.9
c>b>d>a	0.7 + 0.1 + 0.4 + 0.3 + 0.0 + 0.6	2.1
c>d>a>b	0.1 + 0.4 + 0.7 + 0.6 + 0.7 + 1.0	3.5
c>d>b>a	0.1 + 0.7 + 0.4 + 0.7 + 0.6 + 0.0	2.5
d>a>b>c	0.6 + 0.7 + 0.9 + 1.0 + 0.6 + 0.3	4.1
d>a>c>b	**0.6 + 0.9 + 0.7 + 0.6 + 1.0 + 0.7**	**4.5**
d>b>a>c	0.7 + 0.6 + 0.9 + 0.0 + 0.3 + 0.6	3.1
d>b>c>a	0.7 + 0.9 + 0.6 + 0.3 + 0.0 + 0.4	2.9
d>c>a>b	0.9 + 0.6 + 0.7 + 0.4 + 0.7 + 1.0	4.3
d>c>b>a	0.9 + 0.7 + 0.6 + 0.7 + 0.4 + 0.0	3.3

Bold = order of preference chosen by the group

Figure 11.8: The sums of the preference intensities of the 24 possible collective orders of preference

Saaty's analytical hierarchical process (Saaty, 1980) offers a methodology that allows us to model complex decision situations and to assess the possible options. The procedure was developed to overcome complex problems and is not exclusively designed for collective decisions. However, it is particularly suitable for collective decisions, because of the systematic and transparent procedure and it is in fact frequently applied in group decisions. **Inset 11.5** introduces Saaty's procedure and explains why it is particularly suitable for collective decisions.

Inset 11.5: Saaty's analytical hierarchical process
(Text based on Dellmann & Grünig, 1999, p.31 ff.)

The analytical hierarchical process (AHP) was developed by Saaty at the end of the 1960s and beginning of the 1970s (Saaty 1980). AHP is a method which allows complex decision situations to be structured and possible courses of action to be evaluated in a systematic way. AHP has proved its value repeatedly in management, politics and in many other areas (Dellmann & Grünig, 1999, p. 34). The AHP method is suitable for decisions by individuals as well as in collective decisions and is used in practice for both types of decision.

The three terms in the name of the method give us information about the characteristics of the methodology:

- "Analytical", means that the decision goal is broken down into criteria. The options can be compared with respect to both qualitative and quantitative criteria. The criteria can be weighted. The overall assessment of the options is found with linear algebra.
- "Hierarchical" refers to the presentation of criteria, environmental conditions and options. In AHP, these are always arranged on different hierarchical levels.
- "Process" indicates that the solution of a complex decision problem is organized as a systematic sequence of component steps.

The AHP technique consists of five procedural steps:

1. The model elements are determined. This means defining the variables relevant to the decision. In addition to the overriding goal decision criteria, environmental conditions and options must be included. In order to make a decision possible, at least two options must be available.
2. The problem structure is represented as a hierarchy. The overriding goal is at the very top of the hierarchy, and the options to be assessed are always on the lowest level. The main criteria, subordinate criteria and, if necessary, environmental conditions are arranged on various intermediate levels in the hierarchy. With

the exception of the very top of the hierarchy, each level must have at least two elements. As **Figure 11.9** shows, the elements on the lower levels are hierarchically linked to the elements of the upper levels.

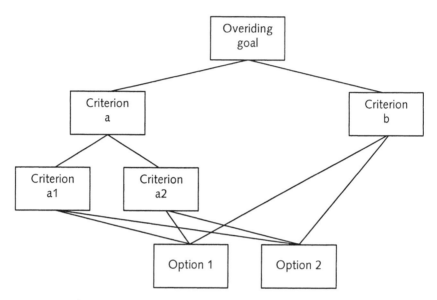

Figure 11.9: Example of a four-level hierarchy

3. Priorities are determined. A priority is the relative importance or degree of influence of an element on a superordinate element. As far as possible the priorities are expressed on ratio scales. With quantitative data which is not measured on ratio scales (for example temperature), and with qualitative data (for example attractiveness) the priorities are determined by means of pair comparison. The relative preferences are produced by comparing pairs of elements in relation to a superordinate element at the higher level, and these are then recorded in a matrix. The Saaty scale, represented in **Figure 11.10,** is used as a basis for this evaluation. The scale encompasses the values 1 to 9 but it also includes the reciprocals from 1 to 1/9 which are not explained in the figure. If the priorities have been determined by means of pair comparisons, their consistency has to be tested. If there is inconsistency, it is essential to repeat the procedure of evaluation. Once a consistent pair-comparison matrix is avail-

able, the vectors of this matrix are determined. This is done by transforming the absolute numerical values into normalized values for which the sum of all the values is 1. This allows data from very different scales to be compared directly.

4. Overall priorities are determined by continuing multiplying and adding of the priorities from the uppermost to the lowest level of the hierarchy. The result of this calculation expresses the relative preference values for the options.

5. The stability of the solution is checked with a sensitivity analysis. This means examining how strongly the result reacts when individual strength of influence is varied.

Value	Definition	Comment
1	equal importance	the two elements are of equal importance for fulfilling a hierarchically superior criterion.
3	slightly greater importance	one element is marginally preferred than the other.
5	significantly greater importance	one element is clearly preferred to the other.
7	much greater importance	one element is very strongly preferred to the other.
9	maximally greater importance	the supremacy of one element is absolute.

Figure 11.10: The Saaty scale
(adapted from Saaty, 1995, p.73)

Saaty's procedure is particularly well-suited to group decision-making for three reasons:

- The modeling in steps 1 and 2 generates a shared view of the problem. In step 1, all group members can bring in the important elements of the problem from their point of view: options, decision criteria and environmental conditions. In step 2, the interconnections between the elements can also be determined in the group. However, the important rule that the overriding goal be placed at the top and the options at the bottom must always be followed.

- The determining of the weightings for the different criteria, the assessment of environmental conditions and the final evaluation of the options in step 3 takes place systematically and transparently. The systematic action stipulated by the method prevents the group from losing its bearings. Transparency requires that the group members must put forward their judgments openly and cannot hide behind the collective. Different assessments are put forward openly and can be discussed fully. Instead of discussing different numerical values, the geometrical average of the individual judgments can be used. This is not optimal, however, as qualitative improvements in the evaluation of the options can usually be achieved as a result of discussion of the differing assessments.

- Finally the AHP method reveals inconsistent individual and group assessment and requires their revision. This can produce a considerable quality gain in the decision. However it requires some tact on the part of the group leader who has to point out to individual members the contradictions in their judgments and ask them for a revised assessment.

In the final subsection 11.2.2 we have recommended measures to make it more difficult for group members to hide behind the group. Saaty's AHP method is one such measure.

Final remarks

"Decision-making is only one of the tasks of an executive. It usually takes but a small fraction of his or her time. But to make the important decisions is the specific executive task. Only an executive makes such decisions." (Drucker, 2001, p. 19).

To make the right choices in key decisions is not only important but also one of the most difficult tasks in management. It is difficult, because such decisions are typically complex in character. This book focuses on complex decisions and sets out to support practical decision-making. After an introduction to decision methodology, the book presents a detailed procedure for resolving complex problems. This procedure divides the search for a solution into a sequence of subtasks, thus making it possible for the actor to proceed step by step in a systematic fashion. The book closes with a discussion of two special issues which are important in practice.

The authors hope that their recommendations will prove helpful for structuring and solving complex problems. They trust that in this way they will have made a contribution to better decision-making, whether in companies, non-profit organizations or government administration.

Index

Bibliography

Arrow, K. J. (1963): Social choice and individual values, New York etc., zitiert bei: Bamberg, G., Coenenberg, A. G. (2002): Betriebswirtschaftliche Entscheidungslehre, München

Asch, S. (1955): Opinions and social pressure, in: Scientific American 1955, S. 31 ff., zitiert bei: von Nitzsch, R. (2002): Entscheidungslehre; Wie Menschen entscheiden und wie sie entscheiden sollten, Stuttgart

Bamberg, G., Coenenberg, A. G. (2002): Betriebswirtschaftliche Entscheidungslehre, München

Bitz, M. (1981): Entscheidungstheorie, München

Blin, J.M., Winston A.B (1974): Fuzzy sets and social choice, in: Journal of Cybernetics Nr. 3/1974, S. 28 ff., zitiert bei: Rommelfanger, H. J., Eickemeier S.H. (2002): Entscheidungstheorie; Klassische Konzepte und Fuzzy-Erweiterungen, Berlin etc.

Brauchlin, E. (1990): Problemlösungs- und Entscheidmethodik, Bern

Bruhn, M. (2001): Relationsship Marketing, München

Buzzell, R.D., Gale, B.T. (1989): Das PIMS-Programm, Wiesbaden

Capgemini (2004): Business Decisiveness Report, London 2004

Dellmann, K., Grünig, R. (1999): Die Bewertung von Gesamtunternehmensstrategien mit Hilfe des Analytischen Netzwerkprozesses resp. des Analytischen Hierarchischen Prozesses, in: Grünig, R., Pasquier, M. (Hrsg.): Strategisches Management und Marketing, Bern etc.

Drucker, P.F. (2001): The effective decision, Harvard Business School Pressl (Hrsg.) Harvard Business Review on Decision Making, Boston

Eisenführ, F., Weber, M. (1999): Rationales Entscheiden, Berlin etc.

Feigenbaum, E. A., Feldmann, J. Hrsg. (1963): Computers and Thoughts; A collection of articles. New York etc., zitiert bei: Klein, H.K. (1971): Heuristische Entscheidmodelle; Neue Techniken des Programmierens und Entscheidens für das Management, Wiesbaden

Gäfgen, G. (1974): Theorie der wirtschaftlichen Entscheidung, Tübingen

Grünig, R. (1990): Verfahren zur Überprüfung und Verbesserung von Planungskonzepten, Bern etc.

Grünig, R. (2002): Planung und Kontrolle, Bern etc.

Grünig, R., Kühn, R. (2005): Process-based strategic planning, 3rd edition, Heidelberg

Gygi, U. (1982): Wissenschaftsprogramme in der Betriebswirtschaftslehre, Zofingen

Haberstock, L. (1982): Grundzüge der Kosten- und Erfolgsrechnung, München

Heinen, E. (1976): Grundlagen betriebswirtschaftlicher Entscheidungen, Wiesbaden

Hill, Ch.W.L., Jones, G.R. (1992): Strategic Management, An Integrated Approach, Boston

Hungenberg, H. (1999): Problemlösung und Kommunikation, München etc.

Kahneman, D., Tversky, A. (1982): The psyhology of preferences, in: Scientific American, 1982 , S. 160 ff., zitiert bei: von Nitzsch, R. (2002): Entscheidungslehre; Wie Menschen entscheiden und wie sie entscheiden sollten, Stuttgart

Klein, H.K. (1971): Heuristische Entscheidmodelle; Neue Techniken des Programmierens und Entscheidens für das Management, Wiesbaden

Krelle, W. (1968): Präferenz- und Entscheidungstheorie, unter Mitarbeit von Dieter Coenen, Tübingen etc., zitiert bei: Rommelfanger, H. J., Eickemeier S.H. (2002): Entscheidungstheorie; Klassische Konzepte und Fuzzy-Erweiterungen, Berlin etc.

Kühn, R. (1969): Möglichkeiten rationaler Entscheidung im Absatzsektor unter besonderer Berücksichtigung der Unsicherheit der Information, Bern

Kühn, R. (1978): Entscheidmethodik und Unternehmenspolitik; Methodische Überlegungen zum Aufbau einer betriebswirtschaftlichen Spezialdisziplin, erarbeitet am Gegenstandsbereich der Unternehmenspolitik, Bern etc.

Kühn, R. (2003): Marketing, Analyse und Strategie, Zürich

Kühn, R., Fankhauser, K. (1996): Marktforschung - Ein Arbeitsbuch für das Marketing-Mangement; Bern, Stuttgart und Wien

Kühn, R., Walliser, M. (1978): Problemdeckungssystem mit Frühwarneigenschaften, in: DU 1978, S. 223 ff.

Laux, H. (2002): Entscheidungstheorie, Berlin etc.

Little J.D.C. (1970): Models and Managers: The concept of a decision calculs, in: Management Science 1970, S. B-466 ff.

Minsky, M. (1961): Steps Toward Artificial Intelligence, in: Procee-dings of the Institute of Radio Engineers January 1961, S. 8 ff., zitiert bei: Klein, H.K. (1971): Heuristische Entscheidmodelle; Neue Techni-ken des Programmierens und Entscheidens für das Management, Wiesbaden

Parfitt, J., Collins, B. (1968): Use of Consumer Panels for Brand-Share Prediction, in: Journal of Marketing Research May 1968, S. 131 ff.

Popp, W. (1968): Einführung in die Theorie der Lagerhaltung, Berlin etc.

Porter, M.E. (1980): Competitive Strategy, New York etc., 1980

Porter, M.E. (1985): Competitive Advantage, New York etc., 1985

Porter, M.E. (1991): Towards a dynamic theory of strategy, in: Strate-gic Management Journal Nr. 1/1991, S. 95 ff.

Ramsey, F.P. (1931): The foundations of mathematics and other logic essays, London, zitiert bei: Bamberg, G., Coenenberg, A. G. (2002): Betriebswirtschaftliche Entscheidungslehre, München

Rommelfanger, H. J., Eickemeier S.H. (2002): Entscheidungstheorie; Klassische Konzepte und Fuzzy-Erweiterungen, Berlin etc.

Rühli, E. (1988): Unternehmensführung und Unternehmenspolitik 2, Bern etc.

Russo, J. E., Schoemaker P. J. H. (1990): Decision Traps; Ten barriers to brilliant Decision-Maiking and how to overcome them, New York etc.

Saaty, Th.L. (1980): The Analytic Hierarchy Process, New York etc.

Simon, H. (1966): The Logic of Heuristic Decision Making, in: Rescher, N. (Hrsg.): The Logic of Decision and Action, Pittsburg

Simon, H. A., Newell, A. (1958): Heuristic Problem Solving; The Next Advance in Operations Research, in: Operations Research Jan.-Febr. 1958, S. 1 ff., zitiert bei: Klein, H. K. (1971): Heuristische Entscheidmodelle; Neue Techniken des Programmierens und Entscheidens für das Management, Wiesbaden

Stelling, J.N. (2000): Betriebliche Zielbestimmung und Entscheidfindung, http://www.htwm.de/ww/teachware/profst/zue.pdf, 08.07.-2002

Streim, H. (1975): Heuristische Lösungsverfahren; Versuch einer Begriffsklärung, in: Zeitschrift für Operation Research 1975, S. 143 ff.

von Nitzsch, R. (2002): Entscheidungslehre; Wie Menschen entscheiden und wie sie entscheiden sollten, Stuttgart

Weibel, B. (1978): Bayes'sche Entscheidungstheorie, Bern

Zwicky, F. (1966): Entdecken, Erfinden; Forschung im morphologischen Weltbild, München etc., zitiert bei: Brauchlin, E. (1990): Problemlösungs- und Entscheidmethodik, Bern

Printing and Binding: Strauss GmbH, Mörlenbach